Switch the Bitch

**MY FORMULA TO BEING
THE CHAMPION OF YOUR LIFE,
NOT THE VICTIM**

PETTIFLEUR BERENGER

Copyright © 2015 Pettifleur Berenger.

All rights reserved. Printed in Australia. No part of this book may be used or reproduced in any manner whatsoever without written permission except in the case of brief quotations embodied in critical articles or reviews.

For book information, see **www.pettifleur.com**

National Library of Australia
Cataloguing-in-Publication entry

Berenger, Pettifleur, author.

Switch the bitch : my formula to being the champion of your life, not the victim / Pettifleur Berenger.

ISBN 13:   9780980411263 (paperback)

Subjects: Self-actualization (Psychology) in women.
Self-realization in women.
Women--Life skills guides.

Dewey Number: 158.1

Cover design by Burst Creative.
www.burstcreative.com.au   Phone: 03 9800 0001

Typesetting by Power of Words.
First published in 2015 by Power of Words, Queensland, Australia. Printed by IngramSpark.
www.powerofwords.com.au

This book is dedicated to all those amazing women trapped in a vicious circle of anger and loss of self-respect; unable to give themselves the true happiness they deserve by taking control of their emotions.

It's never too late to change.

Personal Dedication:

Because you encouraged me, and said "I can't wait to read your book."

- To Cheryl Simonds

Note to Reader:

Although this book is based on fact, people's names have been changed to protect the parties concerned.

"Every single woman has a bit of bitch in her. Who begs to differ?"

-- Pettifleur Berenger

Contents

Preface i
The Switch Definition 1
The Switch Purpose 5
The Switch Formula 11
The Average Bitch Rewards 15
The Nagging Bitch 19
Making the Switch 37
Resisting the Switch 55
The Family Switch 61
Photo Gallery 70
The Bitch Slip 77
Switch the Jealous Bitch 85
The Emasculating Bitch 97
Switch the Enabling Bitch 105
Enrich the Bitch, Make the Switch 119
Ditch the Bitch 127
Respect the Bitch 141
The Sibling Rivalry Switch 157
Older Bitches–Nobody Does it Better 165
Embrace Your Joy, Make the Switch 169

Why Bitch?

When we use the word "Bitch" it evokes strong negative feelings from both the user and the intended victim. My purpose is to take back the power of that word and to positively own it, so that we remove any "victimising" stigma for good.

Preface

When people used to look at me, a lot of them saw the outside, the glamorous surface, and believed all was perfect—hardly! In fact, my biggest weakness was needing acknowledgement: I wanted the reassurance I didn't receive as a child. So I became a slave to this. The more I wanted it—the less I got it. Does this sound familiar to you?

I based my happiness on outside acknowledgment. Then I learned for myself that I am the only one who can give me fulfillment!

Many women crave compliments for their beauty and credit for their hard work to feel complete within themselves. But if you master the technique of simply letting go and being steadfast and powerful inside, this new confidence is more sexy and beautiful to anyone, whether in a relationship, marriage, workplace, or parenting. It generally works in all kinds of relationships.

I had encountered true Passive-Aggressive behaviour towards me. The only way I knew how to handle it was to let my emotions get the better of me. I wouldn't cry, that to me was considered being weak; instead I would get angry. This might display as outbursts, big sighs, or hands-on-hips-narrowing-my-eyes to issues I had no control over. The difference now is, I consider that that behaviour attracted the opposite of what I really wanted.

After years of talking to other women about their relationship ups and downs, learning and observing, I realised that many women have relationship problems due to their whiney, overly aggressive, or clingy type behaviour.

One day sitting down to lunch with a couple of girlfriends, we were discussing several stories of women's crazy, bitch behaviour and came up with the idea that we should write a book about several of these types of bitch behaviour. I found myself repeating the word "switch" this behaviour many times until I blurted out to my girlfriends "we need to switch the Bitch". At that very moment it was like I heard a voice inside my head say "this is your book

Preface

title" and I excitedly announced to the girls that the book should be called *Switch the Bitch*!

The response to the name was received with a bit of apprehension by one girlfriend in particular; she feared the title, however the other girlfriend raised her glass to me in total agreement. The name "Switch the Bitch" was born and there was no way I was letting it go.

After a period of back and forth trying to write this book with my girlfriend, we realised that the writing style and message was not cohesive. Regrettably we decided not to proceed with co-authoring. This was a hard decision to make, but after giving it a lot of thought and losing lots of sleep, I knew it to be right. I am passionate about sharing my formula with others and it was very important to get it out clearly. I felt so committed to writing this book, especially as it sat well with my own life's journey and experiences I had shared with other women.

As I was writing the book, I was testing the formula with real life experiences and keeping notes on the stories. I was excited and blown away by the rewards I was receiving while testing this formula. I also had the communication lines open with friends that were going through issues in their life and constantly testing my formula.

Switch the Bitch

Sometimes it was the friends' problems that helped me to see my own. I decided that it was time to stop and take control of my emotions and take charge of my life and destiny. This in turn gifted myself with peace, joy and happiness — and this attracts all that I need without having to demand anything. I feel loved, respected and eternally happy. Ever since my switch, my family home has been quieter, happy, and more relaxed.

I got what I always wanted… by learning to *Switch the Bitch!* I sincerely hope my book, dear reader, will help get what you need and deserve too.

– *Pettifleur Berenger*

✂   ✂   ✂   ✂

Acknowledgements

First and foremost, I want to thank my son Trent for editing my entire book when I needed another pair of eyes to make it perfect; his brilliance I trusted completely. I want to thank my family for their love and support, especially the man in my life and my three sons: the reason I get out of bed in the morning.

I'd also like to thank Jennifer Lancaster for the great job in organising to get this book self published, the exquisite interior design, typesetting and checking every element. You have been incredible to work with and I couldn't have done this without you. Peter King for the graphic design of my book cover; you understood my vision for the brand.

With special thanks to my dear Lucy Laurita Leielagowns Designer, for your spectacular gowns and friendship. No words can express my gratitude. Thanks to Harry H&H Jewellery Australia for my Switch THE Bitch jewellery. Andrea Agosta Designer Jewellery, Fame Agenda, Dizinof Australia, Mon Bijou, Om Nom Desserts at Adelphi Hotel, Sophie Costello for Photography inside the book; Courtney Crow for Profile Photo.

Above all, I want to thank the remarkable women who have shared their stories with me.

Switch the Bitch

CHAPTER ONE:

The Switch Definition

"I love to see a young girl go out and grab the world by the lapels. Life's a bitch. You've got to go out and kick ass."

– Maya Angelou

Switch the Bitch

Before we begin, let's clearly define and then reclaim full, clear ownership of that previously pejorative term that has sparked so many of our classic battles: Bitch.

When we reclaim this word we effectively defuse all of its demeaning, belittling, or more commonplace connotations as a misogynistic insult. We take away others' power to use it as a painful, dismissive verbal lash intended to wound our psyches and keep us under the thumb. And when we reclaim our ownership of it we effectively "flip it" to wield this term as our own shield of empathy, understanding, and, ultimately, power.

When I use the word "bitch", the woman I'm referring to is not nasty, malicious or a fool. She is not our sexual competition nor is she anyone's social

The Switch Definition

rival or everyone's problem. When I talk about "the Bitch", I am speaking of the inner-bitch within all of us. I'm referring to "the pathetic bitch", "the psycho bitch", "the jealous bitch", "the emasculating bitch", "the nagging bitch", and the list goes on and on. Some of us can relate to being more than one of these and some have experienced being all of them and maybe a few more.

And I'm sure, as you read on, you'll recognise some of these bitches in the mirror! You will no doubt see them all around you as well.

We own that term and we own it free and clear.

We need not feel afraid to face up to the weakest versions of our most powerful selves; just as we need not fear allowing our most powerful selves to stand up straight and tall. We are feminists and non-feminists, traditional mothers and non-traditional partners. We are business leaders and stay-at-home mums.

We have faced hardship, turmoil and unrest… and we may continue to do so. So we must seize control of our emotions and take responsibility for our actions.

Let us understand as we move forward that the utterly dismissive effect of this single word occurs primarily because when we as women react to relationship situations emotionally—as is our instinctive "default" setting—we far too often and far too conveniently surrender control over ourselves and our lives to "the man". Thus we give to him all of the attention and control he desires, along with the crucial emotional lever of power and privilege that he secretly demands.

Switch the Bitch, therefore, is about completely connecting with your emotions and learning to *seize and then maintain control* of your thought processes. This total connection and control will enable *you* to more clearly recognise future consequences resulting from your current or past actions. It will afford you the ability to choose between positive or negative decisions and actions so that you can gracefully override your own socially unacceptable responses or any emotional memories derived from painful past experiences.

Using the straightforward, sensible, effective and liberating *Switch the Bitch* formula in this book will allow you to discard your erratic, emotionally-based thinking and then make a positive, empowering shift in all your existing relationships and, even more importantly, your potential relationships.

CHAPTER TWO:

The Switch Purpose

"The most common way people give up their power is by thinking they don't have any."
– Alice Walker

Switch the Bitch

The stories in this book are all true.

Some stories are based on my own experience and others on the experiences of women I've had the distinct honor of meeting. I've enjoyed the pleasure of their company while sharing our feminine experience and wisdom over coffee, lunches, walks, or a glass of wine (and occasionally lots of wine and the obligatory box of tissues) and even those urgent midnight calls that can be emotional lifesavers for us all.

All names, other than my own, have been altered to protect and respect their privacy, the privacy of their families and to maintain our feminine decorum.

Of course, there are countless women dealing with their own emotionally wild rollercoaster rides, who have little idea how to seize control of their own out-of-control lives. I struggled, suffered and screamed through that ride myself, and many of

The Switch Purpose

us know emotional sisters who already own or are currently purchasing tickets. So if you feel like this is your voice and this is your very own story being told…you're right!

The *Switch the Bitch* formula is simple, straightforward and does not involve working with anyone other than your own powerful self and all the wonders that are within you right at this moment. If you're looking for that one person to change your life, look in the mirror!

Our message is plain in its frankness: *you* are the only person who can make you completely happy. Do not expect anyone else to be wholly or even partially responsible for your own happiness. This may mean wiping out all preconceived expectations of your man. When we start analysing why he doesn't do this or that, we fall into the trap of letting our partner dictate our own happiness.

When you believe in yourself, you'll begin to think differently, act positively and move forward with assurance and purpose.

And always remember: if you expect nothing, you will not be disappointed.

This book is written for women by a woman who

has gratefully discovered the formula for personal fulfillment and also for romance filled with fresh steps to the intoxicating dance of love. This simple formula is not an emotional game of chess, a social strategy of self-serving agendas or a callow scheme to trick, tease, blackmail or otherwise mentally or emotionally "control" your man. In fact, this formula eschews any type of aggression as damaging to all involved and ultimately counter-productive.

The primary ingredient of this formula is taking positive responsibility for yourself and your one-and-only life. The primary payoff is getting positive results without having to deceive, demand, dictate or nag for your true heart's desire.

The Switch Formula is one that will serve you with a lifetime of stress relief, along with an emotionally-rich confidence that will sustain you through all of your life's inevitable storms.

Due to the patently upfront nature of this formula, it will also work effectively in all the many facets of your life, whether they be social, professional or personal. This will be an indispensable addition to your womanly toolkit.

This is because making the Switch involves, very simply, taking charge of oneself, sitting confidently within your own chariot and taking firm control on

The Switch Purpose

the reins of your own emotions. It means having the priceless ability and matchless grace to be absolutely happy with your man but, *with a switch of your bitch*, be fully, completely and equally as happy without him!

Simply, it is just this personal change that will make you infinitely more attractive from the inside. This new sense of glowing confidence will then project outward—like a beacon of femininity and power—because *you are no longer being a bitch*; instead you are *Switching the Bitch!*

Switch the Bitch

CHAPTER THREE:

The Switch Formula

"The thing women have yet to learn is nobody gives you power. You just take it".

– Roseanne Barr

Switch the Bitch

The Goal: Be that woman who everyone unfailingly, enviously notices as they instantly wonder: *"What does she have… because I want to know her secret?"*

What all the gentle readers of this book must understand is that this formula is based on my own experience of being that "pathetic bitch" I mentioned earlier.

Like so many of us, there was a time when I was sincerely disappointed in the reflection in my own mirror. At that time I saw my eyes as dull, lifeless, and filled with a profound sense of sadness staring back at me in defeat. In short, my body felt old and tired and my soul felt hollowed out and hopeless. That was me, then.

Now, the results I've been rewarded with from my own journey and discovery of positive thinking and confident action has given me the drive to live my life confidently, freely and passionately. It's also driven me to write this book in the sincere desire to reach forward and touch other women who are currently struggling with their own lost little girl in the mirror.

I, Pettifleur Berenger, believe I've discovered a formula to love and respect yourself, then use your feminine strength to firmly place yourself in a position where *you* are the pilot at the wheel of your own destiny, not merely your man's passenger. As well, you can be the graceful figure of femininity whose radiant, positive energy attracts one and all to your warm core of confidence, just as it effortlessly captivates that someone special.

The *Switch Formula* is not only for meeting the man of your dreams, but also for keeping him continually besotted with the essence of "you" even as he always, and happily, gives his total respect for you, and you alone!

I call it "Switch the Bitch". Please take a long look at me and let me know if it works.

Switch the Bitch

CHAPTER FOUR:

The Average Bitch Rewards

"It is better to be looked over than overlooked."
– Mae West

Switch the Bitch

Picture this.

Elizabeth is entering a party. She is slightly overweight, her ankles are thick and she has very short, dark hair. Her husband holds her hand and tenderly leads her into the friendly gathering. He softly kisses her cheek, looks lovingly into her very bright eyes and introduces her to his new work mates:

"This is my beautiful wife, Elizabeth. We've been married for 11 glorious years and she's made my life complete with our amazing son and beautiful daughter," he proclaims to all.

She smiles and exudes happiness calmly yet confidently.

"Now what does this 'average bitch' have…" you may unconsciously ask yourself?

The Average Bitch Rewards

"I'm taller than her, thinner than her and so much prettier than her", you reassure yourself, all the while feeling that you're missing something essential to the equation.

You're fascinated and perhaps even captivated by her, but that nagging feeling of confusion just won't leave you alone. You become frustrated and even a bit angry with yourself (and maybe even with everyone else).

But have you ever stopped to think:

"Now what's this fabulous bitch's secret?"

I will tell you with unshakeable faith that deep down inside all the layers of doubt and insecurity built up over wasted time and negative past experience, there is an inner-bitch inside you who already has the answer, if only you could simply access her file and download her information.

If so, she would tell you loudly and proudly:

"When you're happy, then Bitch… you're sexy!"

A closer, more intimate examination of the social dynamic would undoubtedly reveal that this "average" woman is not controlling, nor does she dictate or deceive. She is not possessive or insecure, and she is in

> *"... this 'average' woman is not controlling, nor does she dictate or deceive. She is not possessive or insecure, and she is in control of her emotions..."*

control of her emotions because her inner-bitch is shining through for all to see... like a lighthouse of love and confidence guiding her man to safe harbour.

This is merely one of the life-affirming dividends that faithful attention to the Switch Formula can and will produce.

In the following chapters we will begin to examine many of the archetypical, dysfunctional "Bitches" and using real-life examples, we'll objectively assess the specifics of their situations and then offer concrete, step-by-step instruction on exactly how to Switch the Bitch.

We'll examine the problems with a microscope, but using the Switch Formula, we will remain laser-focused on the solutions!

Now let's juxtapose our "average" but fabulously winning woman with one of the most difficult bitches of all...

CHAPTER FIVE:

The Nagging Bitch

"Success is only meaningful and enjoyable if it feels like your own" – Michelle Obama

Switch the Bitch

Here is a typical scenario: at the end of what should have been an exciting evening out with her man, the nagging bitch's emotions are running wild and her mind is racing erratically.

"Why does he leave me behind, to tip-toe in my high heels up the driveway, so that he can rush ahead to greedily get another beer in his hand before I've even made it to the front door?"

Perhaps he forgot to compliment her on how fantastic she looked or even bothered to comment on her new hair colour. Sound familiar?

But what caused this lack of attention? Did she complain in the car on the way to the party about how late he was getting home from his golf... or about how his friends are a bad influence on him... or otherwise bitchily serve him a veritable smorgasbord of complaints based on her own feelings of neglect?

The Nagging Bitch

Have you ever been that nagging bitch?

It's highly likely that as a direct result of her deep-seated feelings of neglect, this particular bitch would've been ill-tempered, uncooperative and almost certainly pouting throughout an otherwise exuberant social gathering.

Her body language probably, albeit unconsciously, announced to one and all:

Stay the hell away from me!

Her mouth was doubtlessly stuck in accusatory nag-mode and aimed in her husband's unfortunate direction:

"You left me behind to walk into the party by myself... you should be holding my hand and entering the party with me... you never pay any attention to me..."

Blah, blah, blah...

When we allow ourselves to see the situation from an objective perspective, is it really any wonder he wants to avoid and escape this bitch?

Our girl may even think she's doing a great job of hiding her anger and frustration, but the dysfunctional disconnection between her and her mate proves that she is not.

As a socially damaging collateral effect, it's a safe

bet that everyone at the party noticed her seething anger bubbling beneath her volcanic surface… even as they actively avoided the fire in her eyes that she wilfully wielded to furiously scorch her man.

What we must begin to understand is that all this acting out bitchiness is in total opposition to that "average" bitch we just noticed sauntering through the door with her man proudly supporting her.

Have you ever admitted to yourself your admiration for the "average" woman, even as you've experienced the challenges and the frustrating, emotional fallout of being the "nagging bitch"? All this angst is in stark contrast to your appreciation of that confident woman with gentle grace and social success.

Now, have you ever experienced *being* this fabulous woman at some point in your life?

If yes, then good. This is a positive sign that you are already, at least occasionally, able to heed your inner-bitch and move forward in an affirmative direction for yourself and for everyone around you. The voice of your inner-bitch is within you, and all you have to do is listen more carefully to the wisdom of her words.

Our Discovery

We've objectively deconstructed the differing patterns of Bitch behaviour and identified the opposing method of "Switching the Bitch" to your own advantage. Our "Fabulous Bitch" has already made the switch. She knows the secret and we can easily understand the results. She is a practising mistress of the *Switch Formula*.

Our "Nagging Bitch", on the contrary, is stuck in emotional limbo, spinning her wheels to disastrous effect… not only for herself, but also anyone unlucky enough to be trapped in her angry orbit.

Switch the Bitch

CHAPTER SIX:

The Pathetic Bitch

"*Nobody can make you feel inferior without your permission.*"

– Eleanor Roosevelt

Switch the Bitch

This chapter is for all of us who have ever unfortunately surrendered our souls to neglect and abuse and so subsequently felt ourselves more dead than alive; dead women walking alone... and bound to remain trapped in our lifeless ruts.

But this book's message is that there is always hope, if and when we make *the Switch*.

Case in point:

Matilda was at the lowest ebb of her dysfunctional, dissatisfying, decaying marriage. She felt herself not only unloved by Godfrey, her husband of over 10 years, but also continually disrespected and at the absolute bottom of his priority list.

She simply could not understand why she seemed

The Pathetic Bitch

so insignificant to Godfrey, when her entire existence was devoted to trying to make Godfrey her priority, and keep him happy.

She did everything for him, yet Godfrey treated her with almost complete disdain, never complimenting her fashion sense, her considerable cooking skills, nor her business acumen. Indeed, after ten long years, she seemed to him to be little more than a vaguely annoying afterthought, and he regularly treated her as a nuisance.

One fateful evening, Godfrey and Matilda were having dinner at home, and she served up a lamb stew that was an offering from a kind neighbour. Matilda took a bite and found the lamb overly salted and not to her taste at all. But Godfrey dug into his portion and declared that this was:

"...the best lamb stew I've ever had..."

Stymied and more than a little hurt by his enthusiastic praise of what was to her such a mediocre dish, Matilda, desperately seeking some sense of appreciation of her own homemaking efforts, petulantly replied:

"I wish you'd give me such compliments when I cook!"

However, this seemingly harmless plea for appreciative support caused Godfrey to instantly and angrily crack. He went ballistic, screaming at her:

"Liar! I always give you compliments... you really can never be pleased and you're always trying to start fights!"

All this before storming off and making his regular announcement that he was "going out".

Over the long course of their marriage, variations of this same dreadful scene had played out time and time again, leaving poor, confused Matilda feeling dejected, isolated and altogether miserable. Immediately afterwards she would usually lapse into a state of deep depression, as despite her innermost hopes their connection to each other seemed to her to be more distant than ever.

But what exactly was her responsibility for this vicious cycle?

When examined objectively, we understand that Matilda was far too easily manipulated by her husband. He neglected her feelings, simply because he believed that there was no need for him to make any effort in order to keep Matilda, and certainly not to keep her happy. Like a faithful dog that can be left alone on any whim, he was sure she would always be waiting whenever he decided to come home.

A Lesson on Being Manipulated

Sister bitches: If you are easily manipulated, your man will assume he doesn't have to give much of anything important to the relationship. He will be more than happy to provide the emotional minimum while eagerly extracting the personally comfortable maximum.

Matilda was a pathetic bitch, and hence Godfrey was able to conveniently pile all his bad behaviour and shift all of the blame onto Matilda's shoulders. She, in turn, encouraged his bad behaviour by chasing after him time and time again, pathetically pleading her case before he was barely out the door:

"I didn't mean to upset you Godfrey… I was only saying I'd like to be acknowledged for my cooking…"

Blah! Blah! Blah!

This apologetic response gave Godfrey an even more tangible reason to self-righteously flee his responsibility. Meanwhile, Matilda helplessly watched him leave, with another hole callously gouged into her heart.

Switch the Bitch

In the case of the "lamb stew" fiasco, it was 7:00pm when he left, and the hours ticked by as Godfrey enjoyed his sanctimonious taste of freedom. In the lingering interim, Matilda was unable to accomplish anything other than neurotically wondering where her husband might be and what he might be doing. After hours of grueling pain, both emotional and physical, Matilda is left an anxious wreck, helpless, hopeless and suffering... with a pain swirling in the pit of her stomach.

By 10:30pm Matilda couldn't take it anymore. She felt physically ill, and so she broke down and called Godfrey, begging him to take her into hospital.

This pathetic bitch has actually allowed herself to become physically sick because of her own misguided focus! This, of course, is a cry for attention and appreciation, or maybe even something as simple as a hug from the man she loves.

While waiting for him to return, Matilda dramatically lays on the floor of her bedroom, wrapped in her robe in a foetal position, hoping somehow that Godfrey will rush into the bedroom to be at her side. This scenario, however, was not to be the case.

Godfrey, to his credit, returned home shortly after the call.

Why the Man Does not React

You see, after years of passive aggression, Godfrey is accustomed to this type of attention-seeking behaviour from Matilda and so blithely ignores it.

Indeed, instead of rushing to her aid, he calmly walks into the bedroom, looks around, but not spotting her, he promptly walks out, switches on the television and watches the football, seemingly contented.

Of course by this time, Matilda was starving for attention from her man, but as a result of his indifference, she slips easily into anger. Her emotions spin even further out of control.

How is it that he hasn't even looked for me?

If he can't find me, why is he not ringing my mobile?

Her conclusion? How heartless of him!

Now she is not only furious and frustrated, but in a great deal of very real pain. So Matilda decides to call a kind neighbour for the assistance and support her husband is so thoroughly unwilling to provide.

Before her neighbour's arrival however, Godfrey finally finds her cowering in the bedroom. He obliviously inquires:

"What the hell are you doing on the floor?"

Now stretched beyond her breaking point, Matilda tells him to "get out". Godfrey gladly takes advantage of this painless escape from his wife's usual "drama" and departs without hesitation.

Abandoned and alone, Matilda's emotional state continues to degenerate into frustration, pain and anger.

Her neighbour arrives at last and seeing her disheveled state, immediately picks her off the floor. She urgently asks her if she requires actual medical care or simply emotional support.

That was the moment when everything came crashing down for Matilda.

She began to sob uncontrollably, hysterically, helplessly screaming out her years of pain and frustration:

"All I want, is to be loved and appreciated...

Why can't I be loved?

What is wrong with me?

I've given up my life to make him happy, why is it that he can't love me the way I love him?"

This was Matilda's true breaking point.

Prior to that evening's meltdown, she had never encountered that type of overwhelming personal weakness before, that type of total emotional and physical collapse.

Yet at that lowest point, she finally recalls that she used to have confidence and was once a strong, stable, capable woman. She had loved herself in the past, but now can't quite grasp how she'd found herself defeated by this utterly lost feeling of anguish and despair.

Somewhere deep inside, she knew that she had to find the strong Matilda that was still within her. She realised she'd given up her identity as a woman, but now she had to stand up and take control of her own life.

The next morning, she further realised that Godfrey had never returned home that night. She was never to find out where or with whom he'd spent his evening.

But the most important lesson that Matilda learned that terrible evening was that she'd willingly surrendered every part of herself to the cold indifference of her man and, in that draining process, lost her own self-respect, her own sense of confidence, and eventually lost nearly all of herself to a relationship gone sour.

Remember Sisters: *When you lose your self-respect, you surrender all control of yourself to the lowest bidder.*

The very best candidate for control of you is YOU!

Remember that Godfrey, whatever his own failings may have been, did not cause nor seek to cure his wife's "addiction to drama". He merely, and perhaps even understandably, took advantage of the weakness she presented to him to make his own position stronger, more secure and much more comfortable from his own point of view.

> *The very best candidate for control of you, is YOU!*

Yet, despite her internal conflict, our girl Matilda was at her core, a resilient, savvy woman. Yes, she did love her man with all her big heart, but her love for him had painted her into a corner of pathetic, unhealthy and distasteful bitch behaviour.

She knew then that she had only two choices left to make for herself:

The power to change her own behaviour.

The opportunity to leave her husband.

She chose to make *the Switch*.

She called her friend Magritte, whom she knew had already "switched", packed a quick bag and then spent a few quality days with her. They discussed her issues and explored her options until she came to understand that she not only had to, but deeply desired to switch her bitch!

And all the while Matilda was staying with her friend Magritte, Godfrey made absolutely no attempt to contact her, to find out her whereabouts or even to find out if she was safe. This was nothing more than standard operating procedure for him and he saw no reason to alter any actions that had proved personally successful in the past.

As a measure of his confident control, he did not even bother to call to confirm if she was still going to accompany him to a very important business function, which they had earlier agreed to attend. It was socially and professionally vital for him that Matilda attend this function to present a strong personal union, however, by this time he was totally unwilling to bend and much too proud to beg. So, despite his slight loss of professional status, he attended alone.

Prior to Matilda's switch, she might have shown her willingness to attend Godfrey's business function by communicating that she really thought it best for her to go with him.

Matilda, for her part, instead carefully nurtured her own health and wellbeing, then returned home after several relaxing days and stress-free nights with a firmer grasp on her emotions and a much clearer vision of her future. She was no longer prepared to accept living in a miserable relationship any longer. She fully realised that the choice was, ultimately, all hers.

The pathetic bitch was ready for the fabulous switch!

CHAPTER SEVEN:

Making the Switch

"Think like a queen. A queen is not afraid to fail. Failure is another steppingstone to greatness." – *Oprah Winfrey*

Switch the Bitch

Matilda's first positive step was to begin to take better care of herself.

Remember Sisters: *if you can't take care of yourself, you certainly cannot properly take care of anyone else!*

To this end, she started looking after herself more and rearranged her own wellbeing up near the top of her own priority list. She went to the gym, she caught up with the girls, she even went out to the theatre and the ballet for the first time in years. She had always absolutely adored performance arts but had regretfully ignored this because of Godfrey's total lack of interest in accompanying her.

Our determined girl grabbed the reins of her own ride and the direction of her journey. And in doing so, she took control of her own physical destiny with enthusiasm, energy and a real sense of purpose. She

Making the Switch

wasn't waiting for anyone else to go along with her for the ride either!

But she skipped one step that she had normally practised with great diligence and discipline.

She consciously did not share where she was going with her husband.

Unless he specifically took the time to ask her whom she was seeing, what she was doing, or what time she'd be home, she simply went about her business of self-maintenance and social pleasure with a calm, controlled, if understandably excited demeanor. In fact, she rarely even bothered to inform her husband of her departure schedule. This was because he had gotten into the habit of paying very little to no attention to her routine, and so she elected to leave his habit undisturbed.

Much to her great surprise, her new practice of self-improvement and social freedom appeared to put Godfrey into his own tailspin.

Suddenly confused by the newfound independence of this previously devoted "pet", he stubbornly struggled to secure his pride, his control, and to manage his now fragile indifference to her. Over the course of only a few weeks, he became more and more verbally hesitant. He was clearly showing frustration at his lack of control concerning his busy partner's activities and his own inability to properly "solve" what to him had now become a marital "puzzle".

His standard body language, however, from permanent frown on his confused face to a new frustrated energy, as his wife flitted about happily without him, was enough for Matilda to realise something. Godfrey was very clearly beginning to demonstrate some pathetic bitch behaviour of his own!

Remember: *When you make the Switch, you may very well get treated to pathetic bitch behaviour from your man… whether he (or you) likes it or not!*

Now, as the clouds of slavish frustration began to clear, Matilda could see her own old, unhealthy behaviour reflected back to her by a confused and frustrated Godfrey. Being the strong, loving woman that she is, she took no joy in his plight.

Godfrey was a tough man, however, Matilda knew this newfound behaviour of hers was not easy for him to handle, and much more importantly, he was her man.

She quickly discovered that she had to strike a new balance, with her own wellbeing acting as the fulcrum of their relationship lever. She further discovered that as long as she remained respectful and loving to her husband, she could indeed create this new balance with—or even without—him.

This was a difficult task for Matilda, and would be for any loving wife. Yet she realised she had to push through this tough time even if her man was perhaps a step slow, because she believed the relationship was worth saving.

As well, she had faith that he could and would catch up.

Now, gentle readers may rush to the conclusion that this is simply some sort of marital game of "tag", some spiteful agenda of payback, or some harmful campaign of revenge. But, fellow darling bitches, this rush to conclusions could not be further from the truth. In fact, as you read on, you'll discover how this seemingly "pathetic" situation transformed into a blossoming respect for one another and a mutually beautiful resurrection of their love for each other.

Positive Results of the Switch

Within just a few short weeks, Godfrey, to her delight, began to be incrementally more attentive to his wife; he notices as she applies her make-up and catches the scent of her perfume as she dresses for the evening.

Matilda, in response, began to walk with more ease, grace and confidence. Their dance of love begins.

A subtle truth is that men read a lot into where we've been (and where we're going) by the way we're dressed when we leave home and even more so when we return home. When you care for yourself and you make the effort to occasionally set your female phasers to "stun", it will keep his mind more than a little occupied with that dazzling version of you. A sexual creature, he won't mind that bedazzlement at all!

Yet this dance is a slow one. So, just as Godfrey had stopped taking notice of Matilda's appearance whenever she transformed into the pathetic bitch, he intermittently picked up his old game of ignoring her new appearance. We guess this is in order to regain the perceived advantage he'd had over the years. Over the course of their long marriage he had perfected how to push her buttons and understood that the more he ignored his wife, the more attention he would receive in return.

But his game was designed and fitted to the pre-Switch Matilda. After *the Switch*, their dynamic was completely changed. Perhaps most importantly, when Matilda began to switch her bitch, she discovered that she wasn't actually seeking his attention anymore and, much to her surprise, she further discovered that she could easily live without it!

Thus time carried on, and so did our girl.

Matilda engaged even further in her increasingly active and satisfying social life and before she realised it, she had completely stepped out from the shadow of her husband. She was beaming her own bright light of confident satisfaction for all to see and enjoy. She rediscovered the spring in her step and reanimated the confident woman that had been trapped beneath the confining layers of the pathetic bitch that had been holding her down.

This transformation takes a strong mind and a strong woman at heart. Matilda did not start off strong, however Matilda was lucky because she had both, along with the willingness to switch her bitch. She had just lost sight of her inner emotional strength under the power and control of Godfrey.

At that critical point in the switch, a weaker mind and a weaker woman may feel compelled to burst out crying:

"But haven't you noticed my new, improved figure… how beautiful I look in these new pants… have you even noticed

these lovely shoes... and what about my perfume... what about...?"

BLAH, BLAH, BLAH!

Darling Bitches: *He can see your lips moving but he isn't yet listening, so don't bother looking for compliments.*

The Switch secret is that those affirmations will come your way without you ever asking for them when you allow your light to shine. This will come when you believe in yourself and trust how you look and feel.

We must repeat that: *trust how YOU feel!*

This is your emotional compass and this will lead you to the confident, positive results you deserve.

Matilda, being once more the savvy woman she always was, simply carried on confidently and calmly being the bright, happy, cheerful partner that she felt she should be, even though Godfrey became increasingly more frustrated and even a bit nasty about her new life and his new wife.

He continued to resist; he resisted acknowledging and accepting her new behaviour by ignoring her even more than he had done previously. This was his own dysfunctional, attention craving, albeit successful pattern from their past... so he stubbornly stuck

Making the Switch

to his old ways, banging his head against the door of her receptive, perceptive but independent life. He vainly hoped to elicit a reaction that he could "handle" through distancing, just as he had "handled" her in their past.

What he received for his headstrong (but misguided) action was the delightful presence of a loving, if busy, wife and supportive partner. For him, the incredibly positive behaviour and reassurance of her love that he was getting from Matilda was becoming too hard to ignore anymore.

As a consequence of the tango they were now *equally* engaged in, the more rational and composed Matilda remained, the more emotional Godfrey became, until his façade of feigned indifference began to crack.

It started firstly with his completely unsolicited questions.

Godfrey: *Where are you going?*

Matilda: *Just going out to dinner.*

Godfrey: *Where?*

Matilda: *In St. Kilda…*

Godfrey: *Which restaurant?*

Matilda: **Don't know yet… maybe Donovan's.**

The relationship worm had turned.

The Formula...

The formula is simplicity itself.

The question has been answered and no further details are shared. These details are NOT revealed, because we want to inspire his curiosity but not feed it. What we want is to have our man wanting to engage us and to become organically interested in what we're doing again.

Men are naturally intrigued by things that they do not totally control. One need only look at their addiction to big boy's toys for further evidence. Godfrey's halting yet increasingly steady flow of questions (which do represent genuine interest) concerning Matilda's schedule is a predictable result of *Switch The Bitch* independence. This is even if the man sounds a tad aggressive in his curiosity.

Sisters, I will tell you why.

Have you sometimes wondered why he doesn't ask you how your day was or what you've been doing, or whom you caught up with?

Ladies, doesn't that make you pissed off that he doesn't seem to give a damn about you and what's going on in your life?

Making the Switch

The real reason, my Sisters, is because *we talk too much!* If we've already given him the entire weekly schedule in one big breathless blast of "blah, blah, blah!", then why would he ask or listen actively?

Have you ever noticed your man's disturbing tendency to completely forget all the vital details of events regarding you or even the children?

Isn't it true that he then fails to recall these times and dates until you remind him again? In this pattern, then you become furious with him because he's forgotten something so important.

Bitches: *that's called verbal overload… and the Switch Formula calls for us to let it go!*

Odds are overwhelming that he never heard us in the first place or, on his best day, caught little bits and pieces of our half-hour rant. Sisters, we need to talk and answer as required, and for the most part, give him information on a *need-to-know* basis only!

Encourage him to ask questions, because when he does, he will undoubtedly remember your answer to his question. You will then find out that he is actually interested in your life and can pay good attention to your schedule.

So reclaim *your man's* interest of *your world*.

Switch the bitch.

Switch the Bitch

> *Encourage him to ask questions, because then he will remember your answer to his question*

In their past relationship pattern, one of the reasons Matilda had slid into the lonely, pathetic bitch state was because she felt she wasn't getting any decent conversation from Godfrey. What she failed to realise was that Godfrey truly had no questions to ask of her, as she was in the habit of continually bombarding him with verbal overload!

Of course he was happier hanging around his buddies, when he wouldn't be subjected to the withering *blah... blah... blah!*

Sisters, I do hope we realise why we need to STOP talking so much.

At this critical juncture in the Switch, Matilda was somewhat disappointed by his dull reactions. But she stayed on course, and pushed through to upgrade her relationship by switching her bitch. Finally, she was rewarded with unsolicited snippets of appreciative behaviour coming from her man.

For example, when Matilda was stuck in her pathetic bitch stage, Godfrey would expect her to cook, clean and be quiet on command, treating her like little more than hired help. Thus, when she walked in one afternoon to the very pleasant discov-

Making the Switch

ery that Godfrey had washed the dishes while she was out having a fabulous lunch with the girls, Matilda nearly fell over herself. Yet she finally realised that the formula was beginning to garner positive results.

Then, just a few days later, Godfrey emptied the washing machine.

Now please remember ladies that Godfrey is the typical alpha male and until that day could not have found the laundry room with a map. Yet he performed this simple act completely of his own volition and without any prompting whatsoever from Matilda. This is what the Switch Formula refers to as *proper, positive, healthy motivation*!

More gestures of appreciation followed.

Back when Matilda was drowning in pathetic bitchiness, she constantly felt the need to take control of most of their social outings, including simple dinners out for two. In fact, one of their weekly "married couple" traditions was going out to dinner on Friday. Inevitably however, when Friday approached, Godfrey made no attempts to book dinner or even make a simple suggestion of a place he might want to visit. Feeling abandoned and at odds, Matilda would have to ask him what he'd like to do. This, in turn, lead directly to his usual passive-aggressive behaviour, followed immediately by his shunning of any responsibility for their mutual dining pleasure.

Depending on Godfrey's mood, he might reply:

"I don't feel like going out... I feel like pasta..."

Even though he knows Matilda dislikes pasta.

Or he might simply tell her:

"Sort it out... I don't really care..."

Of course this had the damaging effect of draining her already low reservoir of energy.

Sisters: You know *we need to be* organised, but that simply wasn't the case with Matilda and Godfrey. And so, pathetic bitch that she was, Matilda put him on her weary back and carried him to dinner.

But when Matilda *switched the bitch*, she made a firm decision and then took the actions of:

1. Putting him down gently but firmly,
2. Saying goodbye with a smile, and
3. Taking off like a jet to the Friday night rendezvous with her BFFs!

Now, what do you think happened?

Matilda proceeded to revel in a supportive, energising evening out with the girls while Godfrey had

Making the Switch

his own way, *solo*.

Consequently it wasn't more than a few weeks before *he asked her* about going out on their Friday date night, something Matilda had ached to hear in the past to no avail. Yet, still unbeknownst to him, the bitch had been switched, so the first time he asked her for a Friday night dinner, Matilda was forced to demurely reply:

"I would have loved to darling… however, I've already made other plans, so please do give me some advanced warning in the future my love…" and all with a loving kiss before rushing off!

Now allow me to explain why Matilda turned Godfrey down.

Ladies, we beautiful creatures need time for our fabulous selves. We like to be organised, we enjoy the luxury of preparation and as such, we need our time to be respected.

Remember: we are not doormats that can be tossed on the floor and walked all over for anyone else's convenience. By setting boundaries on our time and availability, we will in turn gain the respect we require and deserve.

Once Matilda was fully committed to switching her bitch, Godfrey's irresponsibly poor behaviour began to "magically" disappear. She was getting results.

Switch the Bitch

> *By setting boundaries on our time and availability, we will gain the respect we require and deserve*

I understand that some sisters may feel a sharp impulse to say:

"*F**k you shit-for-brains, you ignored my feelings and now here's your payback!*"

Bad idea, ladies.

Hold yourself together with grace, love and an open heart and don't degenerate into crazy bitch mode. That type of vindictive behaviour can and will deposit you directly back into the pathetic bitch state. When you *Switch the Bitch*, your rewards are peace, calm, happiness, respect and love from all around you. These are the rewards we desire and they are always more than enough.

Being true to her Switch, our girl Matilda continued to live a happy and calm life. She felt no need to nag Godfrey, nor did she desire to do so, since taking good care of oneself can require a great deal of time and energy, leaving little time on our schedules to waste on unproductive power struggles.

Godfrey, stuck in his past behaviours, planned a futile last ditch attempt to salvage his past control, going out on his own one Friday in order to spite her, to play a game of tit-for-tat with his wife's outing.

Making the Switch

In response… she offered him no response.

She didn't ask him where he was going or who he might be going with, something Matilda the pathetic bitch had always done without fail and completely without success.

Instead, she replied with a cheerful, supportive voice:

"Have a lovely time darling!"

And upon his return she graciously greeted him with:

"I hope you had a lovely day!"

Following this event, Godfrey started telling Matilda when, where and who he was with… and what he ate… and what he talked about… and *blah… blah… blah!*

He subsequently instigated a new tradition of date night in advance, and began to assertively choose the restaurant for their evening, making sure to give Matilda's choice top priority.

Matilda *switched the bitch* and let go of her anger, her frustration, her nagging and, ultimately, her heartache.

Today she remains a beacon of calm and contentment and enjoys assured control of her future.

Seize Control of Yourself

Sisters, this story is just one example of the Switch Formula success.

Seize control of yourself and *switch your bitch.*

Matilda switched and she switched her relationship of doom and gloom to one of brightness and mutually supportive, everlasting love. We all can do this and we all deserve it.

CHAPTER EIGHT:

Resisting the Switch

"A woman is like a tea bag – you never know how strong she is until she gets in hot water." – Eleanor Roosevelt

Switch the Bitch

The difficult road, Sisters, is that there is no doubt you will be treated to some level of resistance from your man when you make *the Switch*. He, like so many men, may be uncomfortable with change; he may understandably be thrown at first by your new behaviour, and will undoubtedly make every effort to remain in the comfort zone he has firmly established for himself.

As a result of his initial resistance, we face our own danger of slipping back into being the pathetic bitch if we waver in our commitment to the Switch. We can label this period *"resisting the Switch"*.

So let's examine, using our earlier example, the pattern of resistance we may well face when committing to the Switch.

Godfrey is completely unaware that Matilda has switched her bitch and, as she has not placed any requests *or demands* on him, consequently he goes about his life as he normally would, padding his comfort zone while carefully pushing the relationship envelope.

In this particular example of resistance to the Switch Formula, Matilda was out having lunch with her girlfriends while Godfrey was also having lunch with his mates a mere block away.

After her lunch, Matilda unexpectedly decided to pop in and say "hello" to Godfrey and the boys. She did this because she was enjoying a few rewards of her Switch and she wanted to share her pleasure with her man on this mutually convenient occasion.

In addition, she knew that he liked showing her off to his mates. Matilda was a stunning lady with beautiful blue eyes, a full mouth and high cheek bones that could cut glass, so she wanted to give him the opportunity to display his marital prize and take pride in his wise choice. Classy, smart, stylish and sexy, with her new attitude she was beaming from the inside as well. Indeed she was a smashing success at his table and with his boys. She could see Godfrey was thrilled by her presence, which provided her with an additional confidence boost she further enjoyed.

After a lovely drink and chat, however, she felt it best to keep the visit short and sweet, and so she readied to make a graceful exit. She demurely informed Godfrey that she was ready to depart, but he, instead, made the decision to order another drink. Matilda, nonplussed, patiently sat through the drink while growing mildly bored with all the football and boy talk. After his drink, Matilda stood up to leave, but Godfrey, not yet ready, now wanted her to stay until he'd smoked a cigarette, a habit that Matilda disapproved of strenuously. Godfrey, pleased and pleasantly ensconced in his comfort zone, was behaving as he routinely had in the past.

And in the past, when Matilda wasn't taking control of herself and her emotional state, she would obediently linger; all the while her steamy anger slowly building up and her body language taking on all the signals of disapproval of his bad habits and disappointment with his ensuing behaviour. Godfrey would then generally proceed to ignore her and carry on having his good time. This, in turn, would of course irritate her further, and their time together would collapse into bitterness and retaliations.

But since Matilda had *Switched the Bitch*, this time she politely said her goodbyes; all the while Godfrey pleaded for her to stay while he enjoyed his smoke. *Switched On*, Matilda declined this invitation and instead departed with maximum grace. And so, just

Resisting the Switch

a few minutes later, Godfrey called Matilda to repair the minor social rift. She missed his first call, but on the second call she picked up.

Now, Sister Bitches, this would never have happened in the past for two primary reasons:

1. She would never have left on her own.
2. On the rare occasion she did, she would have been such a whiny, pathetic bitch on the way out the door that there would be no chance in hell that Godfrey would've called her... but every chance he'd stay out for hours after she'd returned home feeling miserable.

So overall there was a small reward for Matilda taking control of herself, even if it came at the price of her husband resisting her enlightened behaviour. Then the situation devolved further.

Godfrey, upset by his own feeling of social abandonment, announced the very next day that he wanted to separate!

Matilda, however, did not take this dramatic bait. After all, Godfrey had the somewhat childish habit of making this same request whenever he felt he had not gotten "his way". Matilda, refusing the bait, simply rose above the fray and went about being calm, collected and content.

And, lo and behold Sisters, just a few days later, Godfrey backed off his emotionally immature response to a rather mundane rift, forgetting all about his dramatic demand. He went back to fully enjoying his wife's upbeat, positive and supportive company… where she was patiently waiting for him all along.

CHAPTER NINE:

The Family Switch

"A strong woman builds her own world. She is one who is wise enough to know that it will attract the man she will gladly share it with." – Ellen J. Barrier

Switch the Bitch

There are no more important roles for any of us women than that delicate balancing act of wife, mother and head of household. Yet as so many of us unfortunately know, all of these vitally important family roles far too often get buried by overwork, under-appreciation and just plain neglect all around, including the dangerously insidious element of self-neglect we ourselves bring dutifully to our own tables.

Now in order for us Bitches to get not only the love but also the respect necessary to juggle all these responsibilities, we need to lovingly seize firm control of some basic household rules.

While your children (and maybe your man too) may seem to bristle at firm discipline and no-nonsense guidelines, as fledging adults they actually have a deep-seated need for an authority figure to "show them the ropes". Never fear, they will grow to value your contributions more and more as they mature.

Case in point:

Petula and Frederick were not-so-happily married, with children. Despite her plans, Petula had begun to slip into "pathetic bitch" mode whenever stressed. After a few years of a more or less "typical" marriage, Frederick had gotten into the careless, but nevertheless damaging, habit of regularly arriving late to dinner with his family.

Petula, as pathetic bitch, would then call Frederick several times to ask how late he'd be, repeatedly betraying her annoyance with each call. Eventually, after he'd finally made it home slightly tipsy, as part of his careless habit, they'd all sit down to dinner with differing degrees of discomfort and frustration, not to mention hunger.

By that time, given his less-than-cordial state, of course Petula would quickly degenerate into being full-on pissed off:

The dinner she spent much time and effort preparing is now over-cooked, the children are starving and squawking, and the fire is building behind her eyes. Her body language sends him a clear message that her pissed state is no act, and the dining table has now become an emotional minefield!

Switch the Bitch

What Petula has failed to grasp is that, as an active pathetic bitch, she's totally surrendered her power to his evident neglect.

Frederick, afraid now of making another misstep, is not game to open his mouth and invite her hostility as he can easily sense from her "dirty looks" and sharp body language that she is far from happy. But, perhaps due to his tipsy state, the silence and the evil eye become unbearable and eventually Fredrick speaks; a big mistake that turns into Petula's last straw.

Boiling over, Petula is eager to lose her marbles and so flies into the rant she feels primed for and more than entitled to…

"Dinner is the same time every day!

You should be using your watch!

You have no consideration for the children or me!

All it takes is a simple call to let me know what time you are coming home so I can organise our dinner!"

And of course:

"You just don't appreciate all the love I put into all this, just so you can have a home-cooked meal waiting for you!"

Ladies, I am sure some of you can agree that we have perfected this routine of venting. This is typically how we women roll when our emotional floodgates are thrown open. We give our all and when faced with inconsiderate family stragglers, we get pissed with everyone around us. So, everyone around us suffers.

But what Petula and a lot of women fail to see is that we too often work around everyone else's whims while ignoring our own schedules and commitments. Thus we subconsciously inject a powerful dose of neglect to our own family situation.

Organising yourself around anyone else is Switch Taboo!

To gain and maintain the respect we deserve, we must seize control of our family schedule, organise our family life around ourselves and then everything will much more easily fall into an orderly place that benefits all. In short, do not shirk your own set schedules… and take control!

What you Must do to get the Rewards

When your man doesn't call, your mind will usually go through a variety of completely unproductive scenarios involving where and what he is doing and why he isn't doing the thing that you want him to do. But in exactly the same manner, when our Bitch is Switched, his imagination will run wild when he doesn't hear from you for a long while. This will allow him to appropriately understand his role in terms of matrimonial responsibility; more judiciously grasp the error of his own ways, and so prompt him to call you.

Short message Sisters: *stop calling your man!*

He is quite capable of getting home on his own without our direction, and we are not doing any favours for ourselves when we attempt to micromanage grown men.

Frederick, quite reasonably following her harangue, wasn't at all keen to return home to face a firestorm after all. From his point of view, they were nagging bitch calls. Even in his disheveled, drunken state, he's quite accurately assessed that he is in no small trouble and then decided, with the help of more than a few adult beverages, that he may as well have his fun rather than get his balls chopped when he returns home.

In Petula's mind she is at least assured of the righteousness of her position and, in fact, believes

The Family Switch

that she's completely right. She feels she's done all the hard work, and all the father of her children reasonably had to do was show up for the family dinner on time, instead of hanging out at his club drinking with his usual clique of mates.

The larger picture she fails to see, however, is that her outburst has only achieved the effect of causing Frederick to stay out even longer, and in his view, gave him valid reason to do so. This has caused Petula to devolve into anger and frustration, subsequently serving up a very awkward, disappointing dinner to her entire family.

When we *Switch the Bitch*, we get the respect from our family that we deserve. We also get the results we truly desire, without blindly stumbling into all-out war with an "enemy" we love… at a cost we cannot afford to pay.

Now let's look at this very simple, unfortunately common problem from the Switch angle.

> *"When we Switch the Bitch, we get the respect from our family that we deserve."*

Frederick fails to arrive on time for dinner. Petula has a schedule and dinner is on the table promptly at 6:30 PM.

Switch the Bitch

She makes absolutely no calls to Frederick, trusting that he is a grown man and knows the time dinner is served.

She, instead, sits down to dinner very calmly with the children and proceeds to have a lovely meal followed by enjoyable conversation. She is relaxed and her children are satisfied. Since Frederick is not home at the end of the family meal, she serves up his dinner and puts it into the oven to keep warm.

When Frederick arrives late after a few drinks, Petula greets him with a warm hug and kiss and says to him in her best cheery voice:

"Hi Honey, I hope you had a wonderful day… The children are in bed and your dinner is in the oven… Enjoy darling!"

And then she scurries off to leave him to his meal and his peace. Frederick, famished after drinking, sits down at the table by himself and eats alone, relieved if somewhat thrown by his free pass and his command of an empty battlefield.

Petula is calm, content and in total control of her evening's destination. She further understands that she has no need whatsoever to waste time with pleading phone calls in the future and can release that particularly unproductive burden forever.

These results are the byproduct of Petula taking control of her own time and family's schedule, and presenting Frederick with the gift of not having to return home or into a lion's den of hunger and resentment.

Frederick, for his part, may or may not be enjoying eating on his own. This is because he sees that his wife has made herself busy with a fresh after-dinner routine; taking the liberty of running herself a lovely, warm bath. He begins slowly to understand on a subconscious level that a fundamental shift in the family dynamic has taken place without him.

After a few weeks of enjoying his enhanced freedom, but growing increasingly weary of his lonely dinners, Frederick realised for himself that he actually doesn't enjoy total silence at the dinner table and he began to relearn his appreciation for the fortifying presence of his family's loving company.

Entirely on his own, he began to arrive home promptly and *on schedule*, where he is faithfully greeted by the smiling faces of his beloved offspring and a very delighted Petula.

On Petula's part, it took little effort or emotional pain to train her inner-bitch, make the crucial switch, and as a result, recover extra leisure time for herself and quality time for her family.

Switch the Bitch

Taking in the Melbourne city views

Off to the Theatre

Switch the Bitch

Relaxing, my home, my space

Put your best foot forward

Switch the Bitch

High tea anyone?

City life

Switch the Bitch

Enjoying some inner calm

CHAPTER TEN:

The Bitch Slip

"It's never too late – never too late to start over, never too late to be happy." – Jane Fonda

Switch the Bitch

Even though we can see right through the trap of our emotional drama stirring within as we devolve into the "crazy bitch", part of the stimulus for this dysfunctional behaviour is that we seem to have this uncontrolled tendency to enter a place of damaging, almost irreversible behaviour, and subsequently feel victorious by inflicting pain on our mates.

Now remember, we like to push the envelope on occasion ourselves and try to get away with as much as we can. There is a part of us that enjoys pushing our partner's buttons just to see how much we are really, truly loved, perhaps because we erroneously feel that this emotional "proof" will smooth over our own insecurities. Once we commit to the Switch, however, the healthiest way to set boundaries with

The Bitch Slip

your man when he's feeling the urge to test you is by controlling the stream of your own attention. In his dysfunctional state, an overly emotional reaction, even if it comes in the form of negative attention towards him, will be perceived as a reward for him.

In the case of Frederick and Petula, weeks after Petula's Switch, Frederick casually announced to her one day:

"I'm going to see my sister for a couple of hours..."

Petula replied with a pleasant "OK", but this contradicted the turmoil she suddenly felt, despite her efforts at emotional control. Her emotional turbulence quickly reached a feeling of abandonment and she reverted to feeling undesirable, bordering on self-loathing, thinking:

"Why didn't he invite me?"

This was Petula's weak point. When these emotions began to unconsciously stir, she would typically react badly.

Of course most of us women tend, from time to time, to be prey to our emotions and so our man will be able to push our emotional buttons once he finds where they are. Yet if we can manage our reaction or even our overreaction, then he will generally be the

Switch the Bitch

more vulnerable one in the relationship.

But this was where Petula, lacking the proper objectivity and surrendering her control too easily, slipped back into pathetic bitch mode.

Only a few hours later, Frederick was all dressed up in his best business suit and prepared to walk out the door to "see his sister…" Petula's weakness, coupled with her ability to see through his bullshit, raced into top gear.

She opened the whine:

"Why are you wearing a suit to see your sister?"

This is a pointless type of question; it is very unlikely that Frederick is going to change the suit.

He nonchalantly replied:

"I felt like wearing a suit…"

Petula implored:

"It's a Sunday and you're just going to see your sister at home… why the suit?"

Frederick offered, even more casually:

"Oh… there's going to be some people…"

Then Petula lapses into desperation:

"So there's going to be a party?"

He demonstrates his impatience with the line of questioning with short answers and an irritated tone of voice.

"No, just some people…"

She finally explodes with sarcasm:

"So you are going to see your sister while she just has "some people" over?"

Our feminine power is lost the moment we start asking questions, because the most vital message that Petula just relayed to Frederick was that the terms of the conversation are now completely his to dictate. He feels like wearing a suit, so just let him wear the darn suit!

Now her emotions are spinning out of control, as she feels certain that Frederick is off to some secretive gathering without her. She's also feeling unwelcome and unwanted. Nor is she completely buying his "sister" story. In short, she has almost totally lost control of herself and slipped her gears back into pathetic bitch mode.

Petula may well be on to something, however she can't change the current situation, just her reaction to the situation.

Frederick, indifferent to her emotional distress, is

halfway out the door while Petula stands by with more questions, but he is, of course, focused on his clean getaway.

In this case it was no more than five minutes before Petula called Frederick, already in a downward emotional spiral of suspicion, veering rapidly toward crazy bitch state. At the last moment, however, Petula desperately controls the tone in her voice and calmly says to Frederick:

"By the way, if you are planning to have dinner with your sister, please do… as I'm off to dinner with my friends myself…"

Because Petula was lurching into crazy bitch state, she transparently and pathetically offered up this fallacy for the sole reason of pissing Frederick off.

Think about it girls, have you ever invented a totally fabricated tale just to make your man jealous? I'm sure I have, and some other crazy bitches have done as well!

But Frederick, mind now on the road, pressed forward:

"As I said before, I am not staying for dinner and I'll see you in a couple of hours… Do you want to join me?"

The Bitch Slip

This was Petula's explosion trigger. Giving in to her emotions, she replies sharply:

"It's a bit too late now, and get this through your head, I will never go out with you or anyone else for that matter unless I have been invited and I will never ask for an invitation either!

Petula was clearly hurt; however, when her emotions took over, she lost her self-possession. Then Frederick effectively ended the conversation by heading out the door.

Now, have you ever had to fabricate an excuse to cover a white lie you used strictly to get your man's attention? This is crazy bitch territory indeed!

So when Frederick returned three hours later, Petula feigned illness and lied that she had to cancel dinner with her friends.

Yes, Petula was hurt by the exclusion, however she had no control over how Frederick might behave. The only person she could control is herself and her own emotions. When you switch the bitch, you stop playing these games.

Silence in the face of emotional adversity is where the power lies!

If Petula had been in control in the moment

> *Silence in the face of emotional adversity is where the power lies!*

Frederick offered the olive branch of a belated and inappropriate invitation, instead of her pride taking over, Petula would have gotten the attention she was really after by simply saying:

"*Yes, darling… that would be lovely.*"

I am willing to wager that Frederick would likely have turned around at once or, forgoing that, she at the very least could have found out his true intentions and uncovered his plans.

But Petula, to her credit, was still able to take a modicum of control back at the last minute because she recognised her own bitch slip. If she were still a pathetic bitch, she doubtlessly would have continued her destructive behaviour when Frederick got home, causing an untold amount of ongoing animosity and adding to his list of perceived grievances.

CHAPTER ELEVEN:

Switch the Jealous Bitch

"Love is like quicksilver in the hand. Leave the fingers open and it stays. Clutch it and it darts away."
– Dorothy Parker

Switch the Bitch

Have you ever found yourself in a situation where you've been ill-treated yet somehow end up in the role of the perpetrator?

This can only happen after you've lost respect for yourself and lost control of your emotions.

Case in point: Bridgette and Dexter

Bridgette is a tall, beautiful, knockout in her 20s with long raven hair down to her waist, soulful blue eyes, and a body most women would die for and most men kill for.

Yet she has one crippling deficiency in her relationship with her long-time boyfriend, Dexter (who is not great looking but a total powerhouse when it comes to emotional control). Despite her killer looks and outward show of confidence, she is in fact desperately insecure with concern to Dexter and their

Switch the Jealous Bitch

relationship. In short, she frequently transforms at the drop of an emotional hat into a jealous bitch.

Whenever your man, intentionally or unintentionally (it really doesn't matter which) makes you jealous, it is not necessarily all his fault. There is usually blame enough for both of you. But when you choose to play the jealousy game, he definitely wins all the emotional reassurance and, in his mind, this proves that you care about him.

In this case, a situation that may seem familiar to many, Dexter and Bridgette were out to dinner with friends when halfway through dinner Dexter gets a text from the dreaded ex!

As Dexter makes a move to fetch his glasses to read the message, Bridgette stole a glance of the name and immediately demanded of Dexter:

"Why are you still receiving messages from your ex?
And why do you still have her number in your phone?"

Not unreasonable requests, we might all agree.

Dexter, however, simply if somewhat lamely replied:
"She's a friend…"

And off they went to the races.

"She's not a friend; you should not be having your ex-girlfriends names in your phone... You demanded that I delete all my old boyfriends off my phone, so delete her name!" Bridgette demanded rather reasonably yet frantically.

To which Dexter retorted, with calm finality:

"I will not delete her name off my phone!"

Bridgette promptly saw red and lost all control of herself. All their friends picked up that something unhealthy was going down. Bridgette continued nagging Dexter about how unfair it was for him to demand that she delete her ex's number... while he continued to unfairly insist that he need not do the same.

Dexter, comfortable with having the upper hand in their relationship and used to getting his way even when he's in the wrong, is confident that Bridgette will lose control of her emotions when pushed. He's well aware that she'll then regress to playing "the naughty girl" who ends up apologising for her bad behaviour regardless of any justification.

So Dexter takes action that he knows will work because it's worked so many times before, and promptly ditches Bridgette at the dinner table. Bridgette, as she so often has before, rushes after him. He angrily fends her off and shuts her down while she, of course, ups the ante by hounding and ranting at him all the way to his car.

And of course the fact that they're both, by this time, intoxicated only adds to the ugliness of the drama.

The fight then carries into the car and all the way to his house as she continues her hopeless nagging and her futile bid for attention. The only reaction she receives in return is cold silence in the car all the way to Dexter's home, eventually followed by the final harsh words to Bridgette:

"Get out of my house!"

Despite the avalanche of words on her part, the big question she is unable to ask or answer is:

What exactly is Bridgette really pleading for in this situation?

Seen from an objective point of view, Bridgette is in desperate need of some attention and just a little love. Perhaps she needs a hug or she just wants him to say: "Bridgette, you are the most important person in my life and of course I'll delete my ex's number if it makes you happy."

However, because she's stuck in "jealous bitch" mode, this not only did not happen but also could not happen, given her out-of-control emotional state pitted against his strong sense of control. Instead, Dexter simply switched on the television, got even more comfortable on the couch and proceeded to completely tune out Bridgette's tired drama.

What did this spiralling "jealous bitch" then decide to do?

She walked over to the balcony and placed her leg over the balustrade, stepping directly into "psycho bitch" territory! Now this was not only a terribly dangerous thing to do in her condition but also, although she couldn't possibly understand it at the time, a childish and completely ineffective way to deal with her frustration. But, desperate for attention and stuck in crazy bitch zone, she would do anything to get his attention.

Dexter, now repulsed by her antics, completely ignored her, not even looking in her direction. Luckily for her that night, she somehow managed to pull back from her emotional gorge and, rather than keep going over, crawled off to bed in shame. Dexter did not join her in bed that night.

All in all, a disastrous end to their evening out.

The next morning, Dexter was still angry with Bridgette, refusing to talk to her and doing everything in his power to avoid her. The silence was killing her, she had completely lost all her self-respect and so believed that the only way for her to retain her man was to commit the ultimate crime and apologise to Dexter.

She apologised to Dexter in order to engage him in a meaningful conversation. This was the pattern she had used in the past, the only way Bridgette could get him to forgive her for her poor behaviour. Dexter, however, was still angry. With careful verbal gymnastics, he managed to spin the issue around in order to become "the victim" in Bridgette's eyes and make her feel like "the perpetrator". A very neat, effective trick that worked for Dexter every time.

From an objective perspective, Bridgette's behaviour was so wrong in so many ways:

- *She displayed zero self-esteem.* She lost respect from her man through her own actions, just as she had so many times in the past. Sister Bitches, to a man there is nothing more attractive than a woman who has dignity, pride and confidence in who she is! Bridgette not only chased after Dexter when he ditched her at the dinner table, a display of total desperation, she then got into his car, carelessly disregarding safety, and flew into total drama.

Switch the Bitch

She then refused to leave his home even after he'd ordered her out. Shameless!

- *She apologised to him the following day.* This was a clear demonstration of low-to-no self-esteem.

- *She was simply trying way too hard.* A man will usually test to see how much a woman is willing to slog for him, and Dexter did exactly that. He got not only pleasure testing Bridgette to see how hard she will run and how high she will jump, but he also had control!

- *She put her life at risk.* Have you ever been in a situation like this, where you have done crazy dangerous things to harm yourself or others in the name of love? That's called crazy, psycho bitch behaviour. It's the type of drama that nobody needs!

Now, when we make the Switch, we flip the script.

When we switch, we act like the true ladies we were always meant to be; we stay composed, elegant and in total control of what just went down. In this case:

If Bridgette had been the one to treat Dexter to some stony silence on the subject of the ex's issue, it would've undoubtedly allowed Dexter to comprehend his own unjust double standard and so he likely would've deleted the name on his own accord.

Silence speaks volumes when it comes to matters of fair play.

This is how my Switch Formula would work.

> *Silence speaks volumes when it comes to matters of fair play.*

Option 1

When Bridgette questioned Dexter about the ex's text, she got an answer she did not appreciate. Instead of resorting to past behaviour that has never been healthy nor successful, Bridgette smiles warmly, turns to the guests at the dinner table and continues to enjoy the rest of the night as she takes control of her emotions and calmly ignores Dexter's answer. She does not give him the attention he craves for his own poor behaviour.

Option 2

Bridgette and Dexter have the argument, Dexter leaves and heads home. Bridgette stays behind and enjoys the rest of the night with their friends. She switches off her mobile, as she has no interest in dealing with any additional poor behaviour from a temporarily unfair man.

Dexter is now the one who is home alone, thinking of Bridgette and missing out on the night. Perhaps he might even analyse the argument along with his own poor judgment.

When you maintain a bit of privacy and he has to wonder where you are and whom you're with, you are stimulating his imagination.

Option 3

They have the argument; they both leave and return to Dexter's house. He ignores her and does not acknowledge that she is hurt. She gets into a cab and heads back to her own home. She decides it's best if she leaves him to spend the night on his own and so does not contact Dexter. Although difficult to do and sorely tempted to pick up the phone, she instead stays in control of her emotions and maintains radio silence. She gives him time to release his anger, and to think about what his own role was in the argument.

When he is good and ready to talk, she then lets him do all the talking, while she listens silently. She does not interrupt and take over the conversation from him. She allows him to accept and acknowledge the situation.

Ladies, do not interrupt your man when he is trying to apologise!

By interrupting him, you give him a free pass to feel justified in his righteousness. Further, he will see your mouth moving but will hear nothing that you're saying, except for the fact that you have failed to listen to him. He'll then become frustrated because he cannot get through to you and you haven't given him a chance to acknowledge the situation the way he sees it.

Learn to accept the fact that he brought it up by himself and that this is an apology in itself! Some men find it difficult to say "sorry"; if they discuss it with you, then it is more than likely their way of saying sorry.

Switch the Bitch

CHAPTER TWELVE:

The Emasculating Bitch

"Success is getting what you want, happiness is wanting what you get." – Ingrid Bergman

Switch the Bitch

Clarice and Ian were on their second date. They were looking to enjoy a drink and perhaps a small bite to eat. They decided on The Press Club in Melbourne city. On arrival the waitress greeted them with:

"Today we're serving a degustation only."

Clarice then made the minor mistake of answering for both of them:

"We were just looking for a few drinks and a small bite to eat…"

The waitress, nonplussed, directed them to another venue.

What Clarice should have done instead was look at Ian with questioning eyes, so that he might take the initiative, answer the waitress and then make the final decision. But she gave him a free pass by answering for the both of them.

The Emasculating Bitch

We must learn to stop taking control of the man's role! This is especially true when, as a single, you are trying to get to know him.

What Clarice failed to learn in this case is how Ian might have handled the situation and the decision he would then have made for their date. A veritable treasure of vital information was lost.

Is he stingy or a free spender?

Does an upscale menu intimidate him?

Is he comfortable in control?

Is he a problem solver?

And most importantly: *whose needs does he consider first?*

By preempting his role, Clarice has just given away a chance to learn more about her prospective partner.

When asked out on an unplanned date we might simply and politely say:

"I love surprises!" (Whether you do or not!)

By doing so, you get to know his personality and a lot about his character. It is perfectly natural to allow the man to take full control of your date so that you can observe and learn more about him: where he likes to eat, places he likes to visit and things he really likes doing. Get into his world so you really know the man you're dating, a man who may potentially be your husband.

Press Pause on Control

Have you ever been that woman who trained your man to be more like your child than your partner? You've taken the driver's seat when shopping, selecting his clothes, choosing the restaurant, arranging the friends you hang out with, etc.

After a few years of being together, have you ever said to your man:

"You've changed, I never knew you liked/disliked this, that and the other?"

Well, that's because instead of allowing our man to make the decisions, we sometimes tend to take charge of everything on the combined social front, and he just follows. This is because it's easier for some men to sit back than take the lead. So he goes to your choice of parties, restaurants, your movie choices, and does all the back seat driving. Remember that he did not fall out of bed one morning and change. He always dressed that way, he always liked his football, his beer, his late night TV and never really liked to

The Emasculating Bitch

hang out with some of your friends and watch Sex in the City with you. Now that he is relaxed in his comfort zone after a few years of marriage, you decide you don't like this person and you nag him to change. Ladies, this is a losing proposition!

> *Remember that he did not fall out of bed one morning and change.*

Have you ever complained about your man never picking the restaurant for your anniversary, nor taking you to a party, a dinner, nor surprising you with a gift? Odds are, after years of following your lead he's simply no longer eager to do it (if he ever was), as he has become much too comfortable in his rut.

He might also assume that you're not going to be happy with his choice of restaurant because it is not your choice and the gift he buys you is not what you want. Because you've been making the vast majority of the decisions in the past, it's unrealistic to begin complaining that he doesn't take you out to dinner unless you make the booking for your birthday or anniversary, or because you're now tired of the extra job on your plate that you created right from the beginning.

Emasculating our man by taking the reins from

him, we are failing to really get to know him. We then become senselessly frustrated and resentful. This is a classic no-win situation for everyone.

When we allow a man to feel that he's genuinely reliable to make decisions and that we appreciate his decisiveness, it makes him feel strong and worthy. Further, it makes him want to be noble and go out of his way to make us happy.

When we switch our behaviour, we enjoy the rewards.

A Case of Appreciation

Joan loved all the gifts she received from Sid. He seemed to unfailingly know just what she loved. Just like we all enjoy compliments, Sid loved being appreciated for his generosity. And all men like to be appreciated for taking care of their loved ones.

What he wants more than anything is to feel valued by you. When you truly appreciate him and demonstrate your appreciation, he will feel driven and eager to give you the world.

You may wonder why Joan received exactly what she loved from Sid. He took her to her favorite restaurants, theatres, movies, holidays, etc.

The Emasculating Bitch

Now let me tell you a secret to getting more of what you want.

Whenever Sid asked Joan what she'd like for her birthday, or where she might like to dine, Joan invariably replied politely and charmingly:

"I would love and appreciate whatever you choose! I trust your impeccable taste!"

This of course makes Sid try his very best to please his lady. Joan, for her part, is not "training" him to be lazy by making his choices for him. Instead she allows him to use his imagination and his generosity.

Remember Sister Bitches: when we request specific gifts, we lose any sense of surprise and so we eliminate from our man the need to put any thought into the gift.

Of course, there's nothing wrong in hinting or guiding your man a bit (or more than a bit). In Sid's case, he made the right decisions because he took it upon himself to take notice of Joan's style, her likes and her dislikes. He paid very close attention to her makeup, perfume, jewellery, fashion style, etc., and he even asked for help from people that were close to Joan, and so he got it right all the

> *Remember: when we request specific gifts, we lose any sense of surprise...*

time. He was the perfect man in Joan's eyes and she was always grateful to demonstrate her appreciation through both words and actions.

Joan was a true lady and by this she got much respect and love from Sid. He in turn was more than happy to put in the effort for Joan.

CHAPTER THIRTEEN:

Switch the Enabling Bitch

"One of the most courageous things you can do is identify yourself, know who you are, what you believe in and where you want to go."

- Sheila Murray Bethel

Switch the Bitch

Here we enter into the inevitable leading-a-horse-to-water phase of the program.

Let's remember, Sisters, that not everyone is ready, willing and able to make positive changes in their life. Nor is everyone open to taking the tiniest swallow of bitter medicine, even if it will surely make him or her stronger in the long run. I believe that prudent application of the Switch theories will lead directly to a happier, healthier, long term relationship with your man, your family and your friends. As well, it will give you a solid base of confidence that will serve you well throughout any of life's storms. But, while its resulting empowerment is universally rewarding and can always be taught and practised, it will not always be learned.

Switch the Enabling Bitch

Sharing *the Switch formula* is one of the great personal gifts we can give to others that will enable everyone around us to flourish in a mutually rewarding environment. However, not all of us are open or prepared to share. Remember, just because an idea, an action or a healthy way of life will be good for us, it doesn't mean that all of us are ready for it!

Case in Point:

Camille is a hugely successful businesswoman, with a lifestyle comfort level that would be the envy of many women worldwide. Her career is soaring, her home is fashionably fabulous, her children are charming, intelligent and well-adjusted, her friends are loving and supportive and her frequent holidays are the stuff that less wealthy women can only dream of. Yet, to her great pain and misfortune, on a personal level Camille has blindly muddled through an adult minefield of one disastrous relationship after the other, and she continues to strenuously avoid opening her eyes as she stumbles recklessly along.

Many of us know women like this and try to help them. Some of us are or have been a woman like this and often reach out for help, but Camille is a woman who appears determined to remain a woman trapped in her own cage.

Switch the Bitch

Her relationship history is at best checkered and at worst, troubling, sad and dangerous. Camille went through a painful, disastrous divorce in her early 30s after a six-year marriage that produced two lovely children. This unexpected divorce, which was pressed by her husband with his infidelity as his primary motivation, seemed to unhinge Camille. It shattered her confidence and sent her into a personal, downward spiral.

As too many of us understand, divorce is a painful tragedy that can humble the strongest of us. But, with time and positive steps in the proper and healthy direction, most of us can walk through the fire and emerge stronger for having done so. Camille seemed to be trapped in the inferno of her personal loss and paralysed with a fear of abandonment.

Reeling from her shock and separation, only weeks after her divorce, she leapt into a relationship with a married man, Larry. Dear Larry held her in limbo for months with what is surely the most unoriginal line in the book:

"I'm going to leave my wife for you and then we'll be together..."

Of course, after months of jumping through hoops for him and finally reducing herself to stalker-type behaviour (even stooping to disguising herself so

Switch the Enabling Bitch

that she could spy on his home undetected whenever he spurned her), Larry had Camille at her highs and lows in a cruel emotional rollercoaster. When he was done, he moved on to his next playmate, still blissfully married of course, and left Camille alone again and twisting in the wind.

Stinging from that slam, Camille then began establishing an ongoing pattern of hooking up with emotionally unavailable types. She soon jumped into her next relationship with Ted, a man in his 20s and more than 10 years her junior.

Ted was full of life, passion and excitement. He was at his most passionate whenever he was helping Camille dispose of her income on lavish dinners and all-expenses-paid holidays (for him). Ted quickly (after only three weeks) entrenched himself in her comfortable home, as and when he wished to take advantage of Camille, and effortlessly took on the role of a "kept" man. He was indeed a kept man who was all too happy to let her pick up all the tabs for his brand new lifestyle funded by her charity.

Although he was emotionally unavailable to Camille, she took on the role of a doting wife. Camille was convinced that they were a delightfully happy couple and she was going to marry him and have his babies, even at Camille's mature age and with her own grown-up children.

After six months of part time, live-in bliss for Ted, and six months of him frightfully draining her accounts, he moved on to greener pastures with a smile on his face and with a brand new car underneath him.

Camille, rocked and shocked again, then set her sights on George. This time, her prospective beau was a reasonably successful businessman who presented a very attractive, reliable front for the entire world to see and admire. Well-dressed, physically attractive, mature and charming, George appeared to be everything she was seeking in a partner. His front, however, soon turned out to be a little more than that and behind that front, Camille painfully discovered that George was a man driven by demons and determined to exorcise them at her expense.

Their relationship quickly and alarmingly became physically abusive. Behind-closed-doors George transformed into a selfish, domineering, jealous and manipulative man who expertly hid an explosive temper behind his charming exterior.

Yet, while Camille's alarms must have been reverberating, she did nothing to extract herself from the poison of this relationship with this frightening man. In fact, after one year of abusive behaviour

Switch the Enabling Bitch

both physical and mental, with consistent neglect, rampant infidelity and frequent break-ups, Camille actually conspired to marry her Jekyll and Hyde!

She was blinded to his bad behaviour and was on a mission to get him to the altar. Camille seemed to be a glutton for punishment and she thrived on attention, even when it was negative and dangerous.

So addicted to the venomous nature of this relationship drug that she aggressively pushed him into the idea of marriage and then pressed the issue until he rather reluctantly agreed. Of course this only freed him to allow his demons to rage not only unchecked but thoroughly approved of by his new bride.

Camille had, in short, made a deal with the devil with her health, her wellbeing, her sanity and her life as the bargaining chips.

Needless to say, this deal did not enrich Camille's life and only served to beat her spirit down over time. As well, it inevitably isolated her socially, as her life became a ceaseless treadmill of scrambling to ignore, evade, excuse or cover up her husband's seemingly endless string of bad behaviour both inside and outside of their marriage.

Due to her husband's often crude, tactless behaviour with her female friends, one by one the faithful women who had supported her throughout all of

Switch the Bitch

her past difficulties were forced to separate themselves from the couple. They were quickly growing tired of George's often lecherous and always inappropriate come-ons that were becoming a common detriment to so many of their otherwise enthusiastic social gatherings.

This is only one of the examples of the damage that poor choices can wreak on our lives, Sisters, yet it is one of the worst forms of losing control.

When we as women not only validate our man's poor choices and abusive behaviour but also go on to allow him to wreak havoc on our social scene, we are left in the role of public defender for his crimes.

> *When we as women not only validate our man's poor choices and abusive behaviour ... we are left in the role of public defender for his crimes.*

And this public defender role is one for which we receive only reluctant cold shoulders and zero replies as our reward. All the while, our perpetrator goes merrily along like a raging bull in a china shop.

In Camille's case, things came to a head when her daughter was invited to a 15th birthday party of one of her closest friends. The party was large and well attended by the mums of the invitees, who had planned the get-together for months.

Switch the Enabling Bitch

It wasn't strictly a female party, however because so many of Camille's friends were gathering, almost all the dads were taking advantage of the "time off" to enjoy a beer with their mates on their own, while the mums dropped the children off at the party and then enjoyed some relaxing drinks and chat time with just "the girls". To that end, the hostess of the birthday bash had tacitly requested that Camille attend alone, in the sincere desire to avoid any social awkwardness for any of the guests. However, for some reason, George manipulated Camille into taking care of another errand. Having chosen to ignore the unwritten rules of the soirée, he conspired to crash the party sans Camille. He was the only husband in attendance.

A certain female guest who had suffered through his advances on previous occasions quickly became the focus of his attentions, along with the abundance of free alcoholic drinks available.

The ladies, who until his untimely arrival had been having a smashing good time amongst themselves, were then forced to deal with the elephant in the room. Needless to say, while they did not allow George to completely ruin their party, he was a constant obstacle to overcome and a handful (or two, with busy fingers) to ignore. This was until he became drunk enough to steer towards a taxi and home.

Switch the Bitch

The following day, Camille received two phone calls of gentle reprimand. One was from Nellie, the party's hostess and Camille's best friend, while the other was from Gertrude, the direct target of George's inappropriate behaviour, along with an embarrassing "FYI" recap of George's performance that both ladies felt was more than overdue. Camille, feeling mortified but inexplicably backed into a corner, refused to trust her friend's good judgment and adamantly denied her "version" of the evening's events. Yet undoubtedly, deep inside, she had little difficulty realising what her husband's shenanigans had cost her in terms of social embarrassment.

This one event caused a chain reaction of broken ties and shattered connections that Camille was too embarrassed to repair, and none of the women felt the necessity to take on, as by this time they had given up on even hoping that Camille would see the light. Instead, they moved forward in their own direction, unfortunately without her.

Although her best friend still reached out to Camille, Camille's good-hearted sense of loyalty to her husband and desperation to be loved by him isolated her even further by putting up walls to close herself in with her man and entrap herself even further in her dysfunctional marriage.

The friendship Camille had with her best friend was one of the most beautiful things she had in her life. They would share everything with each other with a daily morning call, and sometimes a few calls over the course of the day. Nellie gave her all the support she needed through all the turmoil of her past relationships. However, right after the party, Camille withdrew, and over time her very tight relationship with her best friend started to fade.

Nellie was very hurt by the loss of the friendship; even worse, Camille lost a caring and loyal friend to stay in a toxic relationship.

The only person who can save her from this pattern is Camille herself.

Results of Taking the Less Travelled Path

But what could she have done?

Many of us still trapped in our enabling relationships may be asking this.

She could have made *the Switch* from delusional bitch to the intelligent, loving, loyal and strong woman that she was and will always be. She could have faced up to the poison that her man was spreading throughout her life!

Would this have been easy?

It would not have been.

In this case, making the Switch would undoubtedly have caused Camille to *re-examine her relationship and re-evaluate its worthiness for the future.*

It would have caused her to *stand up to her husband and demand that he correct his abusive behaviour and seek professional counselling.*

It would have caused her *much effort to repair the relationships that had been wantonly damaged by her husband's past behaviour.*

It may have ultimately forced her to *seriously consider distancing herself physically or take steps in that direction.*

But what other effects would the Switch have had on her life?

It would have allowed her to step back, breathe deep, set her feet firmly into the ground and re-establish the position in her own life as the attractive, strong, vital, capable and caring woman she is. She would once again be the primary driver of her own destiny.

Instead, Camille still suffers through the day-to-day agonies and debilitating stress of constantly dealing with an abusive husband, while feeling helpless and trapped inside a woefully dysfunctional and loveless marriage.

Sisters, we may not all deserve everything that we get in our lives. But, none of us deserves to sit in the prison of an abusive marriage simply because we lack the strength to free ourselves. We may indeed create our own cages, but we have to realise at some point that we always have the key inside us.

> *"... step back, breathe deep, set her feet firmly into the ground and re-establish herself as the attractive, strong, vital, capable and caring women she is."*

Switch the Bitch

CHAPTER FOURTEEN:

Enrich the Bitch, Make the Switch

"It takes a great deal of courage to stand up to your enemies, but even more to stand up to your friends."
– J. K. Rowling

Switch the Bitch

Creating and/or adding stress to an already unhealthy or stressful situation can often have the opposite effect that we intended as loving, nurturing caregivers. We all need the freedom to make mistakes, even when these mistakes affect our day-to-day health and wellbeing.

Sometimes a step back is a step forward.

Case in Point:

Annabelle met Henry at a friend's party and there was an instant, mutual attraction. Both single and in their early thirties, Henry asked her out and she happily agrees.

Now, Annabelle is a lovely, attractive woman who is very health-conscious and takes great pride in her physical fitness. She works out regularly at her gym, is an avid runner, makes every effort to eat healthy, fully enjoys a social drink when she can and expects nothing less in her mate. Easygoing and even-tempered, her one pet peeve is that she simply cannot tolerate smokers. Upon meeting Henry, he seems the perfect match.

Henry is so committed to his own healthy lifestyle that he retains his own personal trainer who he works out with several times a week, regularly completes six kilometre runs, eats healthy and also enjoys fun social drinks with friends and does not smoke. *At all!*

But, unbeknownst to Annabelle at the time, this healthy lifestyle of Henry's was a complete reversal from his previous circumstances.

Prior to meeting her, Henry had undergone a massive, personal self-improvement program due to a serious health scare. Consistently overweight and fighting the battle of the bulge, Henry had also been a lifelong smoker, starting in his teens. He had neglected all dietary disciplines and had struggled with his self-image and self-esteem because of these issues. This was all before a doctor's visit gave him an alarming wake-up call.

To his great credit, however, Henry had taken control of his life and righted his ship, embarking on a fitness program and making a herculean effort to alter his eating habits. Over the course of a few years, before meeting Annabelle, he had achieved spectacular results. He had given up smoking completely, lost over 16 kilos and had maintained a healthy, satisfying diet that had changed his lifestyle completely.

To Annabelle, they seemed a match made in heaven. Their romance quickly blossomed into a love affair filled with long, happy dinner dates and rich conversation, which led to romantic walks afterward and then to long, romantic evenings together that she cherished. Within six months they were engaged and two years after their first meeting they were married in a joyous wedding attended by their closest friends and family. The marriage quickly transitioned into a loving, supportive, uplifting partnership. They were a popular power couple with a great number of social engagements and connections; for a long while they maintained busy, fulfilling lifestyles both together and separately.

Then, inexplicably, seven years into their satisfying partnership, Henry began to partake in the occasional "social" cigarette at parties, along with his "social" drink. This shocked and infuriated Anabelle, as she was well aware of all the suffering Henry's past health issues, had caused him.

She could not believe that he would gamble with

this serious, unhealthy and very unattractive addiction. To her confusion and consternation however, Henry continued down this slippery slope and slowly began to increase his "social" smoking and drinking over time.

This behaviour really got Annabelle's back up and she would then launch into lectures. This in turn led to recriminations and inevitable frustration for her as Henry, perhaps emboldened by her tickings-off, slipped further and further back into his old destructive habits.

In fact, within just six months, Henry had regressed into his full-blown smoking addiction. Along with this seriously unhealthy habit, he also lost interest in his training and running, and began to replace his diet with poor, unhealthy choices, escalating quickly to a shocking weight gain. Drinking more and more heavily, Henry took on an overall bloated appearance that broke Annabelle's heart.

She found it increasingly difficult to be near him, even when he wasn't smoking, and their relationship began to suffer from lack of affection. Shocked and more than upset about the rapid, physical degeneration of her man, Annabelle spent quite some time banging her head up against Henry's self-destructive walls until she came to a difficult but clear decision.

Switch the Bitch

She had to *Switch her Bitch* and distance herself from her husband, no matter the cost!

Annabelle came to the healthy conclusion that all her caring, all her pleading, all her attempts to help him climb out of his own hole were to little avail, and that her husband was unfortunately determined to plunge further into his downward spiral. This was despite her best efforts to help pull him out of it. She had to make the Switch and refocus all her energies on the one thing she could control: herself!

So, dismayed with her partner's decline, angry and frustrated with him and herself, she pulled back and allowed him all the freedom he required to do whatever it was he wanted to do with himself, despite her natural tendency to help her man.

- She abandoned the lectures, the pleading and all her disapproval and simply let Henry go his own way. When he went outside for a smoke, she said nothing and ignored him.

- After dinner she simply allowed him to indulge in his habit as she went about her normal routine, even though she missed his conversation and company.

- She continued to pursue her own fitness goals by herself and made no effort to try to rope Henry into joining her or doing it on his own.

Enrich the Bitch, Make the Switch

- She refused to complain about the smell of the smoke, the expense or the long-term effects (i.e. nagging) and simply went her own way, enjoying her life as she had before, only now with the new challenge of enjoying it essentially alone.

Annabelle, to her good fortune, quickly discovered that this hurdle was not at all difficult to leap. In no time, she re-discovered a passion for her health and fitness and began to fully engage in her own productive lifestyle, all while cutting Henry loose from any responsibilities she felt concerning his health and welfare.

As months passed by, Henry began to approach Annabelle and engage her in conversations about the dangers of smoking, coyly mentioning his own efforts to cut back, even as he continued smoking. He frequently asked if she had noticed how many cigarettes he'd smoked, as if hoping for her to notice that he had cut back. She did not take the bait. Her usual response is a patient, loving:

"Well, Darling, please do as you like… you're a grown man after all…"

Usually issued right before she dashes off to do her own thing.

Switch the Bitch

Now Sisters, we do wish that this particular account could have a happy ending… but in the real world, men will be men and boys will be boys! While Henry has in fact come around to Annabelle's way of thinking regarding a healthy diet and is trimming down, he still seems unable to get the cigarette monkey off his back. Although, to his credit he has reduced the amount and frequency with which he smokes.

Annabelle carries on looking fabulous and full of life and love as she sets a healthy, attractive example for her husband to enjoy.

We can lead our horses to water Sisters… but that doesn't mean we can get them to drink it… no matter how badly they need it!

CHAPTER FIFTEEN:

Ditch the Bitch

"Love yourself first and everything else falls into line. You really have to love yourself to get anything done in this world."

– Lucille Ball

Switch the Bitch

Now let's examine one of the most heartbreaking of all dysfunctional relationships, one we all have some form of experience with, either first or second hand: that dismal, one-sided, uphill battle between *the emotional player* and the *woman-with-permanent-blinders-on*.

Irish-born Hilda, a medical professional in her early 20s, hooks up with the doctor of her dreams, Mubarak, an Indian born, extremely handsome, charming man with impeccable taste in all things exquisite. Ten years her senior, Mubarak woos Hilda on the job, playing to all her secret fantasies. A whirlwind romance develops. Although Mubarak is at times unavailable both physically and emotionally, she graciously chalks it up to his profession (although hers is equally stressful), closes her eyes and plunges wholeheartedly into this relationship swimming hole.

Falling madly in love with him, they manage to remain, in her mind at least, a committed couple in a relationship of one year duration. This is despite some unnerving signs along the way, which are entirely apparent to Hilda, who chooses to make excuses for him in her head. His availability was always on the spur of the moment when he had a spare couple of hours to spend with her. Yet, she was content with the scraps he fed her, and all in all, the year had been blissfully happy for Hilda… she was sure that she'd found "the one": her perfect soul mate. Then, in the midst of all this coupled-up bliss and *seemingly* out of nowhere, Mubarak drops a bomb on all the dreams that Hilda's been harbouring for a year, blowing them to pieces.

With no hint of any prior background knowledge offered, he announces to her one day that he'll be returning to his native homeland to get married to an Indian woman. This arranged marriage orchestrated by his parents is calmly explained.

He further informs her that he'll be leaving in just seven months to seal this pre-arranged deal and marry this mystery woman. Emotionally floored by this knockout punch out of nowhere, Hilda pleads for further information and at least some explanation—but Mubarak coldly stonewalls her. Their first "break-up" commences.

The pull of passion and close professional proximity quickly becomes too much for both, and so they begin a game of "on again/off again". This has all the convenient adult benefits remaining in place for him in the present, and all the emotional pain for her immediately afterwards.

Finally, distraught and emotionally strung out, she summons her last shred of confidence and decides that she can't see him anymore. Hilda requests from him:

"Just don't even tell me when you're leaving because I can't stand to know… just leave and that will be it between us…"

He accepts these very manageable conditions and shortly thereafter, adhering to the unspoken schedule, departs for his homeland and his first marriage.

Hilda, distraught, torn up and struggling to keep her chin up, finds herself in such pain in the subsequent weeks that she then decides that she needs to get away from all the now painful Ireland memories of their love gone wrong, and so plans and executes an entire career and logistical lifestyle switch to Melbourne, Australia.

Within the three months following Mubarak's departure, Hilda heroically manages to resettle her entire life and career in Melbourne and slowly begins a fresh start. Then her phone rings.

Is it Worth a Second Chance?

It is, of course, Mubarak calling from India, with suddenly passionate pleas of:

"I miss you... I can't live without you anymore... I called the wedding off... I have to see you again... I'm moving to Sydney to be closer to you..."

Her aching heart soars with romantic hope all over again. She believes his sudden reversal without question and in the subsequent weeks they rekindle their romance cross-internationally through very long distance phone calls and emails. They make new plans of a romantic reunion in Australia in their immediate future, complete with a "fresh start" for both of them. The big day of his Sydney arrival comes at last.

But to her confusion and regret, she receives no call, message or email from him to confirm his arrival on Australian shores. She assumes that he is exhausted from the long trip and gives up on reaching him

Switch the Bitch

after more than a few failures to establish contact.

As days pass, there remains no word from him on his Sydney status or otherwise. She commences worrying:

What if he didn't make it?
What if he's been delayed?
What if…

Finally, unable to stand the terrible suspense anymore, Hilda contacts his new workplace. They inform her that he has, in fact, reported for duty but is currently unavailable to receive phone calls. Embarrassed, she hangs up in a state of confusion. Then, that evening she gives in to panic and calls the new Sydney home number that he's previously given to her.

A woman answers.

Off balance but undaunted, Hilda asks to speak with Mubarak and the woman calls him to the phone. Hilda's heart is racing at the very idea of speaking to him again. They're now finally within reasonable travel distance to each other and her spirits soar as he takes the receiver. And that's exactly where they crash.

Hilda questions with curiosity:

"Who is the woman answering your private home line?"

Mubarak immediately cracks it! He coldly and brutally berates her in no uncertain terms:

"You have no business calling me… what do you think you're doing? Why are you even calling here… I don't want to speak to you!"

Then he ends the call with an unceremonious hang-up. She collapses in tears, an emotional wreck of shattered dreams and wasted love, once again discarded in the relationship bin like so much used trash.

You would think this is where it all ends, but no.

The following day, he calls her back to assure her that the previous evening was:

"a big mistake… a huge misunderstanding… a one-night stand… totally inconsequential… it's you that I love…"

Hilda, after her long night of tears and previous let-down, is more than somewhat dubious, but somehow she still retains a spark of hope. They end the conversation with him making promises to visit her in Melbourne and her listening carefully, however non-committal.

They then begin calling each other and months pass as they begin a new shorter-distance phone relationship wrapped around both of their busy schedules.

After three months of this, he calls and passionately, frantically, joyously announces to her that he'll be visiting Ireland for a medical conference for one week and that he would like her to join him there where he can finally, officially meet her parents and where he can officially profess his love to her and, last but certainly not least, they can then get "officially" engaged.

Sister Bitches, *if you're beginning to sense a pattern here, then your BS Antenna is properly tuned for womanising men!*

But young Hilda swallows the bait with her whole heart, her primary question to him being about the Ireland accommodations. He tells her not to worry because, he states: *"I will take care of everything…"*

He further explains that he'll have to first check into his hotel and attend the first of his meetings at his conference before he contacts her. But then he cut off the call, failing to provide any further details, albeit reassuring her all the way that he'll *"… take care of everything…"*

Over the moon with joy and hearing impending wedding bells, our girl books an appointment at a wedding planner and actually proceeds to pick the wedding dress of her dreams, which she is sure she'll need in the very near future. After a good deal of joyous shopping around, she finds the dress of her dreams and then proceeds to purchase it and take it home to wait for the big day!

The Ireland holiday week soon approaches but Mubarak has still managed to relay no further details, so, stuck in travel limbo and in an emotional tailspin of entirely her own creation, she desperately calls an Irish friend and asks if she can bunk at her place for a night, or a few nights if necessary. Now, openly flying blind into a Bermuda Triangle of a holiday, she takes leave off work, books a flight and hauls her life to Ireland to wait for his call, which she is sure will be forthcoming. And, in fact, he does finally call her... but upon hearing of her Ireland status as "arrived", he quickly begs off actually meeting up. His excuse is that he's *"too tired from the conference"* but promises her that he'll call her tomorrow after a good night's sleep.

The following day he does call, they meet for dinner and afterwards for an adult evening back at his room.

During their dinner and throughout their reunion however, there is no talk of meeting her parents, no proposal or even any talk of a wedding proposal. Our girl, drunk with romance, doesn't dare have the nerve to bring it up because she doesn't want to spoil their "reunion".

Their romantic Ireland "holiday", to her dismay, turns out to be only that one night however, as he continues to claim to be "… too busy with work…" to see her anymore that week. Instead, he leaves her abandoned in Ireland and twisting in his emotional wind.

This is time, Sisters, and *long past time to ditch the bitch.*

And that Hilda did!

Hilda returned to Melbourne very angry; her love had turned bitter.

Her first point of call was the Bridal store. She walked in with her head held high and requested a full refund of her bridal gown payment. On refusal of a refund, Hilda took the Bridal shop to VCAT (court) and she won. A small victory for the heartache and pain she had suffered. Well done, Hilda!

Point Number One. When any man makes an announcement that he's going to marry another woman, it's time to cut that relationship clean and let it drift

Ditch the Bitch

away with the tide. Weak sauce Sisters may beg to claim:

- *But it was an arranged marriage and he didn't really want to do it...*
- *He's just under a lot of pressure from his parents and so...*
- And of course the old familiar: *It's really me that he loves and if I just keep hanging on...*

> *When any man announces that he's going to marry another woman, it's time to cut that relationship clean and let it drift away with the tide.*

EVERY SINGLE ONE OF THEM COMPLETELY, UTTERLY, TERRIBLY WRONG! Not only that, but every one of those excuses is also deeply misguided. Why? Because of point number two...

Point Number Two. What this man is intentionally planning and cleverly choosing to do is to play an *emotional game of Relationship Chicken.* He has decided to test Hilda's devotion by driving his power of control over the relationship head-on and at full-speed into her love for him, knowing her dreams of a fulfilling marriage, in an effort to see who will deviate out of the way first in order to save the both of them.

This game of *emotional chicken* is similar to the game of *emotional blackmail* in that once we give in to the demands (and these are *demands*, not requests nor choices) we are doomed by default to a lifetime of always giving in to *any and all future demands*.

In other words:

Hilda has completely surrendered any hope of having any sense of control at all moving forward!

Which leads us to this.

Point Number Three. This is a dysfunctional relationship in a constant state of applied pressure and emotional blackmail, being dominated by a man interested primarily in *manipulation, control* and ultimately, *power*. Power over *you* and power over *your relationship* with every calculated play designed with the express purpose in mind of consolidating that power and squeezing the last drop of resistance out of you. This isn't love, Sisters, it's *emotional torment*.

> "This isn't love, Sisters, it's emotional torment."

We'd be better off suffering through the initial sting of a tragic break-up rather than the lingering agony of a torturous relationship. And the evil metaphor is—very unfortunately—

apt here. Because this type of emotional manipulation bestows on its victim a slow, chronic, draining state of emotional agony, sometimes with brief periods of remission and hope, but it is one that ultimately debilitates before it completely destroys.

Switch the Bitch

CHAPTER SIXTEEN:

Respect the Bitch

"When one door of happiness closes, another opens; but often we look so long at the closed door that we do not see the one which has been opened for us."
- Helen Keller

Switch the Bitch

At a certain age, most of us in our modern world of instant connections, casual hook-ups and even casual divorce have to come to grips with a certain amount of complexity regarding our relationships. For better or worse, for the foreseeable future, divorce is a very adult reality, and the complications that inevitably crop up as a result need to be as gracefully managed as possible if we have any hope of enjoying mature relationships.

Men especially, but certainly not exclusively, are prone to racking up track records filled with the odd divorce or three, along with all the complicated familial relationships that follow, before they get their own matrimonial setting dialed in properly. Of course this means that as mature women seeking mature men, we often have to deal with not only the reality but also the long-term responsibility that comes with caring for children from previous marriages/relationships. This can be a windfall of joyful communion, a hard road

Respect the Bitch

of bitter servitude, or almost anything in between these extremes, which is what it most often turns out to be when we accept the love of a good man as well as the loved ones that are his forever. Naturally that arrangement goes both ways.

One of the complexities that we often have to deal with —that can be infinitely trickier than even the presence of maturing children—is the ongoing, hit-and-run presence of the often-dreaded ex-wife. Although not always poisonous outside of their natural habitat, this mysterious breed of female can be manipulative, possessive and alarmingly needy all at the same time and often demonstrates little regard for her former mate's current associations.

Case in Point:

Nancy and Denzel met in their late 50s, when the handsome, worldly, successful entrepreneur and all-round alpha male swept Nancy off her feet.

After a short courting period, they both decided to move in together in order to move the relationship to the next level. Their next level turned out to be filled with happiness and mutual satisfaction for both of them, but it also included Denzel's teenage son from his first marriage, Dudley. It was a bargain that Nancy accepted readily, willingly and lovingly—to

Switch the Bitch

Denzel's great relief—and, upon making Dudley's acquaintance, to her own as well.

What she was less relieved to discover, however, was that the all-new trio's live-in bliss was going to be subject to frequent, unexpected and often ill-timed (or perfectly timed she occasionally thought) casual intrusions from the ex-wife.

Although on the whole Nancy found their domestic bliss a blessing, as time went by, she began to chafe at Denzel's willingness to allow this woman from his past into their home at the drop of a hat. To Nancy's way of thinking, Ms ex demonstrated little regard for scheduling ahead to announce her frequent visits. As the ex-wife adamantly refused to be in the same room as Nancy, and Denzel gave in to this demand, her visits were more than a little inconvenient for Nancy to say the least.

Denzel would ask Nancy to leave their home or stay in the bedroom as and when required, to accommodate his ex-wife's visits. This would upset Nancy, but to keep the peace, she would obey Denzel's request.

Months flew by and the "pop-in" situation worsened. Nancy, rather to her dismay, felt forced to question Denzel about the frequent visits by the ex-wife, because he seemed to regard the ex-wife as little more than a minor nuisance and rarely skipped an opportunity to indulge her whims.

"Denzel, I would appreciate some respect around our home; I am bothered by your ex-wife's unannounced frequent visits."

"Nancy, you need to stop complaining and put up with her visits. She's the only mother Dudley's got…"

"If your ex-wife does not want to be in the same room as me, she should not put demands on me to leave my home… she should find another option."

"You're being a pain and starting to annoy me," Denzel declares.

"Denzel, you are the only person that can put a stop to her demands, yet you choose to let her rule our lives."

Denzel would not respond and was content to leave it at that, even though Nancy was infuriated. But not wishing to come off as shrewish or selfish, she generally swallowed her frustration and quietly digested it for the sake of the boy and in the interest of domestic peace, even as the ex-wife became more and more demanding.

In addition to the pop-ins, Denzel was required to attend numerous family functions with Dudley and with the ex-wife in tow, functions in which the ex-wife had decided were for the three of "them" and that Nancy was "not welcome". Nancy gritted her teeth and did her best to smile through it. Denzel gave every impression that he was more or less comfortable with the situation as it existed and showed little interest in addressing it.

Within a year of living together, Nancy had had enough and began to openly voice direct complaints to Denzel, which ultimately fell on deaf ears. For her, the situation was becoming untenable. But, as she became more and more openly vocal with her grievances, Denzel became less and less open to even acknowledging them.

Their relationship then began to dissolve into frequent spats, where inevitably Denzel's alpha personality would rear its ugly head and he would harshly dismiss not only her but also the very validity of her grievances. Nancy, intimidated by his much more passionate personality and stung by his strong vigour, was completely unable to match his flaring anger. So she thought it best to surrender all control of her own home to Denzel and his ex wife, in the hopes that her man might eventually come to see her side and rescue what to her was a floundering relationship heading for the rocks.

For his own reasons, Denzel continued to allow their domestic ship to drift.

Respect the Bitch

This established a pattern of Denzel's dominance and Nancy's submission to his will... as well as the flighty fancies of his ex-wife. And so Nancy subsequently lost all her passion for her relationship and its future. But as she was settled into comfortable domestic submission, she did nothing to change the course of her situation and instead simply knuckled under to Denzel's authority. She spent many an evening alone, feeling sorry for herself and wallowing in depression.

Years passed with no real change. Nancy began to console herself with the fact that at least her relationship with Dudley was strong and healthy and that the boy was developing into a fine young man, in spite of any tension he may have gradually perceived regarding his father and her. Her domestic life, once so full of joy and romance, was now little more than a frustrating charade in the hands of seemingly everyone but herself.

Eventually Dudley's 18th Birthday loomed. Dudley himself eagerly and innocently asked her if she might be attending his "big party" at a popular, local restaurant. For Nancy, this was the final humiliating straw. She had not even been aware of the party plans and, of course, Denzel had not taken the time or trouble to inform her.

That night she steeled herself and when Denzel arrived home, she questioned him about the arrangements (for the first time in years). She then reasonably suggested an alternative plan. She announced to him that she would very much like to throw Dudley a separate party at their own home so that they might be able to "celebrate together".

He dismissed this with a casual: *"that won't be necessary, his mother is taking care of all that..."*

But, undaunted, she pressed forward. She began by pleading:

"Denzel, you have the power to change this... you and I could have a party for your son at a neutral place and your ex-wife can choose to attend, as she is welcome, or we can have a party in our home with our friends and your ex-wife can have a party at her home along with her friends for your son... After all, she is the one who has the problem of being in the same room as me..."

Denzel replied bitterly and angrily:

"FINE... then she simply won't come at all... are you happy now?"

But Nancy pressed the issue:

"Denzel, she simply has no right to force you to choose to going to your children's functions without me, as you know I would want you to be with your children... but the

downside of that is that I'm always left out."

From there, the evening quickly degenerated into a shouting match, with Denzel escalating his angry tone:

"Why don't you fix the problem if it bothers you so much?"

Nancy broke into tears.

"Of course it bothers me... of course I'm hurt to be excluded... how would you feel if I did the same thing to you?"

Denzel then angrily pounded his fist on the table and summarily dismissed her as he ended the argument to his satisfaction:

"I'M SICK OF THIS NONSENSE BETWEEN THE TWO OF YOU, SO DO WHATEVER THE HELL YOU WANT!"

He then stormed out of the house. The "argument" was over, leaving Nancy sick, sad and more bewildered than ever before. She simply could not understand why they all couldn't come to some reasonable compromise together, or why Denzel seemed so helpless, allowing his ex-wife to dictate all the terms of every situation, even when he knew that it impacted his relationship with her.

She felt lost and alone.

On the night of the party, the ex-wife arrived, unannounced, to pick them up. Dudley and Denzel dressed in their finest before leaving to attend the party. All the while, Nancy is watching in agony. After Denzel departs, Nancy burst into tears of frustration and unhappiness, alone and bitter over her exclusion from such a significant part of his life and now her own.

But in this case, *what could she have done differently?*

So very, very much Sisters.

A Framework for this Switch

First off, all men (and especially alpha males) appreciate an independent woman.

This may be the secret to Denzel's ex-wife's not-so-strange hold over him --- or it may not. Yet it's clear that there were more than two people sitting at the table when Nancy was dealt some cards in the beginning of her relationship. Clearly there were three players, but only two of them were eyeing their cards, playing their hands, checking, bluffing, betting and raising, while the third was just innocently watching the game unfold before her, although she had all her chips pitched into the pot too!

Divorce and the complexities of divorce are a

reality that we may all need to deal with in one sense or another. But that doesn't mean we have to just sit there and let life roll over us as we learn to play dead!

Nancy could have set some clear guidelines in the beginning of their live-in situation and then made sure that her wishes were respected moving forward. Just as anyone entering a relationship involving children and exes from previous relationships would be wise to do.

A proper framework is always helpful to everyone involved, especially children, to help guide all through the difficulties that will inevitably occur in today's complex relationship networks. Guidelines are essential because when relationships involve children, by definition, this is a long-term commitment that requires proper, respectful boundaries for everyone involved.

Nancy passively forfeited control and further surrendered her independence when she allowed Denzel and his ex-wife to dictate all of the scheduling inside her own home. Denzel's own acceptance of his ex-wife's demands is at best passive/aggressive, and at worst, hints at deeper issues that Nancy may or may not want to face. But, if she truly wants a future with this man, she must face them squarely

Switch the Bitch

and honestly, no matter the consequences.

Her Switch (or anyone else in a similar position) would go like this:

1. *In relationships involving former partners and children, always set firm guidelines* in regards to visitation schedules/rules as well as childcare and responsibilities. Once again, this is not only helpful for the adults but also provides a healthy framework for the children to grow within.

2. *Assert your independence.* Nancy surrendered all her control and passively allowed her partner and his ex-wife to roll over her life while she suffered silently.

3. *Men may not always want to make a choice but they'll always respect someone who forces them to make it.* There are issues with Denzel and his ex-wife that Nancy completely failed to address. These issues may be minor or they may be major, but Nancy should not fear facing them, nor should her partner, who seems all too willing to allow poor behaviour to go on, to Nancy's detriment. This is not an equal partnership and it is not love.

> *"If she truly wants a future with this man, she must face them squarely and honestly, no matter the consequences."*

Respect the Bitch

What can Nancy do Moving Forward?

She must now aggressively assert her independence and *Switch her Bitch*, and then face the consequences of her own previous passivity.

Does her partner conspire to plan social events with his ex-wife without her knowledge? Fine. Move on girl, and go your own way!

She needn't wallow in the mire of her own self-enforced loneliness. Nancy has the freedom to do as she pleases, without the responsibilities of caring for complex social campaigns, so she must accept that freedom with open arms and take advantage of it.

Similar Sisters, you must set your own schedule and do your own thing.

- Meet up with your friends for a girl's night out.
- Take a course in your favorite subject/hobby/activity and then go meet fellow enthusiasts.
- Plan a solo holiday.
- Indulge yourself!

Becoming an independent woman may lead Nancy to exactly the type of respect she deserves from

Switch the Bitch

Denzel and the kind of love she wants, or it may lead to a more mutual understanding and trust between them, or it may lead to an end to their fractured relationship. But she must take action and make *the Switch* — for her own good and for the long-term good of everyone involved.

Nancy knows she must take control of her life and take charge of the situation at hand. So she prioritises her schedule and her needs.

Strong men aren't afraid of strong women, and Nancy need never be afraid to be one.

So Nancy finally took control; she announced to Denzel that she would not be leaving their home or staying in the bedroom during the ex-wife's visits.

Denzel replied: *"She will not visit our son and it will be your fault."*

Nancy ignored the harsh comment and emotional blackmail and stayed in the home. She prepared some snacks and a pot of tea for the ex-wife. When the ex-wife arrived, she had a massive hissy fit and left. Denzel did not waste any time in blaming Nancy for the abrupt departure. Nancy very calmly cleared the snacks and tea and went about her business.

Within just a few months, Denzel and the ex-wife came to terms with the Nancy rules and followed it with precision. The disrespect for Nancy stopped the moment she took control.

After a long absence of the ex-wife being in Denzel and Dudley's life, one evening Denzel dropped one of those hard-to-swallow pills to Nancy, stating: *"I am going to my ex-wife's birthday dinner"*.

Nancy was dumbfounded and bit her lip to stop herself from saying something. She had Switched the Bitch and mastered the art of emotional control, so no attention was given to the recurring battle of the ex wife.

However, the damage encountered from this unacceptable situation had toughened Nancy up. She had exhausted her emotional bank and gone past the point of caring.

Ladies, don't let yourself come to the point of living an emotionless life. Take charge of your life with all the strength and grace you can give yourself *before* you find that your hurt has made you numb to the utter beauty of life.

Switch the Bitch

CHAPTER SEVENTEEN:

The Sibling Rivalry Switch

"The best and most beautiful things in the world cannot be seen or touched but are felt in the heart."
– Hellen Keller

Switch the Bitch

Now we enter the realm of one of the most complex relationships that almost every woman everywhere will ever have to face: *the Sibling Rivalry*.

This relationship is complex for a number of reasons, but we can all agree that one of the primary reasons is that, unlike other non-family ties, the sisterly sibling relationship will undoubtedly last for a lifetime. But we should always remember that although our sisterly blood bonds may go through their ups and downs over the course of a long lifetime, these bonds are some of the very strongest and most loyal that we will ever forge, and these bonds are a gift we must strive to preserve and cherish. In addition, and although it may not always appear so, these bonds are based on the strongest, most faithful love that we as human beings will ever be able to cherish and have the opportunity to enrich our lives.

Complex, confusing and confounding? Guilty as

charged. Powerful, faithful and forever? We know it in our souls, even if we sometimes try to ignore the feeling.

But one of the most frustrating aspects of the sibling relationship is that far too often, while the relationship is mutual, the rivalry is one-sided... although both sides are equally sucked into the dysfunctional vacuum of trying to "win", even when only one side is actively fighting.

Case in Point:

Janice and Erin are sisters.

Growing up under the guidance of their professionally successful parents, they are teammates dedicated to helping each other achieve the same success their parents attained. They encourage each other to claim their role in the greater world of opportunity that they both know exists. To a great degree, they both succeed.

But along the way, as is inevitable when growing up, they chose separate paths to success, and each pursued success vigorously. But Janice, the older sister, upon achieving much that she desired—and outwardly maintaining what most would call "a successful life" filled with economic freedom, a loving husband and healthy family—inexplicably allows a seed of jealousy to grow within her regarding her younger sister Erin.

Erin also enjoys an accomplished life, with the same opportunity and the same comforts of companionship and family that her sister has achieved and that any good woman would cherish.

To the objective observer, both sisters are fantastic examples of self-made women achieving worldly success and fortune. But to Janice's subjective feeling, Erin has achieved just a *tiny* bit more success than she has, and so she allows this to become the bitter seed that festers inside her soul.

Over the course of their adult lives, Janice allows this seed to infect her, until the bitter bloom manifests itself in Janice's inner envy and volatile, outer anger. This anger announces itself on her face for all the world to see, while she casts herself in the role of "victim" before her own mirror. This becomes a face that most people are only too happy to avoid; a victim that no one can help.

But as a loving, caring sister, Erin has no desire to avoid her older sibling, even though over the years Janice has begun waging a bitter campaign of malice and retribution for slights that only she can perceive. Family holidays turn into stress-filled contests of

The Sibling Rivalry Switch

spite and one-upmanship, even when Janice is the only one playing. Their overall relationship degenerates into a one-sided battle of sustained pettiness and arbitrary meanness designed to wound Erin's feelings, damage her psyche and ostracise her from the rest of their family. Erin suffers but doesn't know why?

And this brings us to the most painful aspect of sibling rivalries.

What we have in this case, and in far too many cases, are two sides locked in a losing war, effectively being waged by only one side, contesting control over a relationship that is being slowly destroyed by the side most determined to control it. It is the proverbial case of a woman burning her house down in order to keep anyone else from living in it.

In the end, no one has a roof over his or her head and everyone loses!

Of course the real tragedy with sibling rivalries is that not only do the siblings lose all the love and soul-sustaining support that could have been theirs to nurture through years of one-step-forward/two-steps-back conflict, but the innocent families of both are also forced to endure the hardships heaped upon them by this endless, childishly malicious, self-destructive and self-defeating battle of guerilla warfare. This is the ultimate in stressful, unhealthy and counter-productive behaviour.

In this case, Janice wages her private war, never recognising just how much her younger sibling loves and admires her, and how much she wants her older sister to be a part of her and her family's lives. Heartbreak piled on top of heartbreak!

Yet because Janice has never stopped to reconcile with her feelings, she's never been able to see that Erin has made the Switch, and so Janice can never quite process Erin's non-threatening acceptance of her "losing" position in Janice's battle. And though Janice seems to be committed to her "winning" campaign, she is consistently frustrated by Erin's ambivalence towards engagement in their one-sided conflict. Yet, this ambivalence only catalyses her to redouble her efforts to "win" because her mind, body and soul are short-circuited by anger and envy, and she's mired, firmly and unhappily, in her "victim" tracks.

What happened next?

Family holidays and gatherings became a stressful ordeal for all and a power struggle in which Janice was the only person seeking power, a power that everyone is only too happy to grant her.

The former sibling love turned into sibling use and abuse, as Janice desperately tries to make up ground

The Sibling Rivalry Switch

that only she's felt that she's lost.

Janice became increasingly frustrated over her younger sister's compassionate acceptance of the struggle, while Erin seemed to rise above the fray.

What Janice fails to understand is that Erin has *Switched the Bitch* and understands that she cannot be hurt, because *she will not allow herself to be hurt*. Erin knows that her joy cannot be stolen, because *she will not allow her joy to be stolen* by anyone. Erin knows that she cannot be drawn into bitterness, because *she will not allow herself* to be drawn in. She has made the Switch and is in charge of her emotions, her actions, and she is in charge of her own life's direction!

The once-hurt Erin is *Switched On* and is switched off from her older sister's vindictive behaviour.

> *"The once-hurt Erin is Switched On and is switched off from her older sister's vindictive behaviour."*

Unfortunately, this means that she's unable to help her older sister, who is so locked into her battle that she cannot let it go for fear of losing everything. It also means that unless her older sister can come to terms with her own life, her own emotions and her own direction, she will not be able to make the Switch to truly enjoy all the rewards that she's spent a lifetime earning. A lifetime that is now wasted on a bitter, unhealthy, struggle towards ultimate failure.

We can and must remain strong for our siblings, but we cannot always save them from themselves. Erin continues to love her sister Janice, however she will not engage in the drama.

CHAPTER EIGHTEEN:

Older Bitches — Nobody Does it Better

"The question isn't who's going to let me, it's who is going to stop me" – *Ayn Rand*

Switch the Bitch

Meet Clarence and Clementine. They're a happily-retired couple in their 60s, enjoying their golden years, their large loving family, all the rewards of a long life that they've certainly earned, along with each other's blessed, constant company. A more perfectly matched couple I have yet to see, and a more boisterously fun pair than I've yet to know, who have spent over four decades chasing each other around our wonderful game we call life.

But, ladies, even perfection requires the occasional tweak. As a calm, cool and caring Zen Master of the Switch, Clementine knows exactly how to lovingly tune the dial of blissful companionship as she sees fit.

When sitting down to their supper one recent evening, Clementine graciously served the dinner that she had prepared for the one and only love of her life.

Upon regarding her labour of love, Clarence remarked shortly:

"Sausages again?"

Clementine smiled and continued serving her man before seating herself and enjoying his company (although seemingly ignoring his menu inquiry) then tucking into her own meal happily.

The following evening, and for 29 consecutive evenings, sausages were the main item of every dinner menu. Clarence, being quite endowed with the wisdom of years, thoughtfully never questioned the menu again.

Happiness reigned.

Ladies, Clementine's theory would probably never occur to you as a possibility to make a point. However I am fairly safe to assume that at some point your cooking and housekeeping skills have been challenged. In most cases, due to all our hard work, our emotional button is triggered, we fly off the handle and go off on a tangent. Sound familiar? It does not work ladies!!

So find something that does works in your situation. Perhaps request very calmly: *"I would love your cooking tomorrow darling"*.

Switch the Bitch

We must try to remember some golden rules. The calmer your reaction to all situations, the higher the rewards you receive. Clementine did not have a day filled with built-up frustration, ready to snap at Clarence upon assuming he was suggesting some slight inadequacy on her part. She was a superbitch at keeping her emotions under total control. My father often says to me, "actions speak louder that words"… Clementine obviously agrees.

We must learn to control our flow of hateful words that we so very easily, at the hint of any negativity towards oneself, feel an urge to spit out. Remember bitches: *silence is golden and speech is silver.*

Ladies, the years will be kind to us because we have spent a lifetime in service of our loved ones and, if we can only make the Switch, we will be kind to ourselves.

And so gentlemen… don't mess with us Older Bitches!

CHAPTER NINETEEN:

Embrace Your Joy, Make the Switch

"Life is not measured by the number of breaths we take, but by the moments that take our breath away."
– Maya Angelou

Switch the Bitch

As women we are often referred to as the "weaker sex". This is a term that is no more bothersome than a warm summer breeze, as we Sisters who have lived a life of childbirth, nurturing, loving and caring for our children, our men and our friends understand that along our journey, we've been stronger than we ever imagined we could be. We've also been more loving and caring than we ever thought possible.

Now is the time to embrace the joy of our beautiful existence, to nourish and foster that natural joy inside all of us so that everyone around us can bask and thrive in its healthy, life-affirming splendour. This is our reward and it is a reward we must share whenever and wherever we can.

By making the Switch of your inner Bitch, you can move directly towards this joyful life. It is in this direction where we will be most able to find our highest enlightenment and our greatest fulfillment for ourselves, and more importantly, for our loved ones.

At this point you may be wondering about my personal results. From the core of my soul, I can proudly say my life has never been happier. I don't expect my life to be nourished by anyone except myself, no matter what circumstances I am faced with in life. I've learned to give myself the power from within to overcome any external negative influences that used to dictate my entire happiness. I walk within my story and own it, I stay true to myself, and some people will not like it. But life goes on. I prefer to be beaten with the truth than kissed with lies. I have no shame in apologising; I have found strength in forgiving and happiness followed me in the process. I completely switched my inner bitch and took control of my own destiny.

> *"I prefer to be beaten with the truth than kissed with lies."*

What we can do to Embrace Joy

We can Claim Ownership of Ourselves and our Roles.
We no longer need to be defined by male standards or societal standards. Our roles as women, wives,

mothers and life-givers will define the paths to our own fulfillment, and our paths will be open for all caring human beings to follow.

We can Take Control of our Emotional Life.

We are loving human beings, born to love and care for others, yet we can choose our own emotional forms and settings. We need not be victims or victimised by negativity, stereotypes or emotional dysfunction.

We can Become a Beacon of Calm in a Sea of Life's Storms.

The human world revolves on an emotional axis that no one can control and with a future no one can predict with any accuracy. But we can become the emotional shelter for our friends, families and our partners, who may sometimes spin out of control along with it. And for ourselves too!

We can Discover Love All Around Us.

In all its many forms, we were born and built to create, nurture and sustain love. We will do so with a positive, healthy and nourishing heart for our one and for our all. When we find our love for ourselves, then love will find us everywhere that we go.

Embrace your Joy, Make the Switch

We will Embrace Joy… Always.

We understand that our lives, and the lives of those we love, are meant to be filled with as much joy as we can manage. Too, we will realise that our hearts are filled with an infinite capacity to love. Our joy cannot be stolen, disrupted or destroyed… because we are its inexhaustible source. Our wells run deep and our direction is pure.

My *Switch the Bitch Formula* involves understanding that our initial emotional reactions are not going to serve us; however, actualising some good common sense, positive actions: only this can free us. When we take positive steps to reach out and assert our independence, it is not only for our own health and happiness, but also the health and wellbeing of our loved ones.

Our *Switched On Path* may not always be a smooth ride, but it will always be healthy, peaceful, loving and contain more of the reciprocal love that we as women live for. There is a great power in giving an emotionally healthy love on our joyful journeys to living our best lives and nurturing our greatest loves.

"Dignity will only happen when you realise that having someone in your life doesn't validate your worth"

–Shannon L. Alder

CPSIA information can be obtained
at www.ICGtesting.com
Printed in the USA
LVOW06s1613240816
501582LV00058B/703/P

9 780980 411263